Working with
Drug and Alcohol Users

D1141609

by the same author

Working with Suicidal Individuals
A Guide to Providing Understanding, Assessment and Support
Tony White
ISBN 978 1 84905 115 6
eISBN 978 0 85700 224 2

of related interest

Counselling Older People with Alcohol Problems
Mike Fox and Lesley Wilson
Foreword by Dr. Martin Blanchard
ISBN 978 1 84905 117 0
eISBN 978 0 85700 319 5

Tackling Addiction
Pathways to Recovery
Edited by Rowdy Yates and Margaret S. Malloch
ISBN 978 1 84905 017 3
eISBN 978 0 85700 369 0

Understanding Street Drugs
A Handbook of Substance Misuse for Parents, Teachers and Other Professionals
2nd edition
David Emmett and Graeme Nice
ISBN 978 1 84310 351 6
eISBN 978 1 84642 449 6

What You Need to Know About Cannabis
Understanding the Facts
David Emmett and Graeme Nice
ISBN 978 1 84310 697 5
eISBN 978 1 84642 856 2

Working
with
Drug and
Alcohol Users

A Guide to Providing Understanding, Assessment and Support

Tony White

Jessica Kingsley *Publishers*
London and Philadelphia

First published in 2013
by Jessica Kingsley Publishers
73 Collier Street
London N1 9BE, UK
and
400 Market Street, Suite 400
Philadelphia, PA 19106, USA

www.jkp.com

Copyright © Tony White 2013

All rights reserved. No part of this publication may be reproduced in any material
form (including photocopying or storing it in any medium by electronic means and
whether or not transiently or incidentally to some other use of this publication)
without the written permission of the copyright owner except in accordance with the
provisions of the Copyright, Designs and Patents Act 1988 or under the terms of a
licence issued by the Copyright Licensing Agency Ltd, Saffron House, 6–10 Kirby
Street, London EC1N 8TS. Applications for the copyright owner's written permission
to reproduce any part of this publication should be addressed to the publisher.

Warning: The doing of an unauthorized act in relation to a copyright work
may result in both a civil claim for damages and criminal prosecution.

Library of Congress Cataloging in Publication Data
White, Tony, 1957-
Working with drug and alcohol users : a guide to providing
understanding, assessment and support / Tony White.
pages cm
Includes bibliographical references and index.
ISBN 978-1-84905-294-8 (alk. paper)
1. Counseling psychology. 2. Drug abuse counseling. 3. Alcoholism counseling. I. Title.
BF636.W485 2012
362.29'186--dc23
2012033828

British Library Cataloguing in Publication Data
A CIP catalogue record for this book is available from the British Library

ISBN 978 1 84905 294 8
eISBN 978 0 85700 618 9

Printed and bound in Great Britain by Bell & Bain Ltd, Glasgow

Contents

Acknowledgments

After 30 years of practice how do I start to acknowledge all those who have contributed to my professional development? I was 22 years old when I began to run my first therapy groups, an unusually young age, and as I look back now I cannot believe I actually did it. This early start occurred because both my parents were psychologists. In my early years I had a look at the psychology profession, and found I could work quite well within it, so I started and have never stopped. We worked well together, my parents and I, for 15 years and thus any acknowledgment must start with them. I did indeed learn a great deal from them, not only technical material but how to live the lifestyle of a counselor/psychotherapist. As it's an unusual profession you must learn this or you will not last too long.

Professionally, my other major influences were Bob and Mary Goulding, who taught me how to understand people. Not just how to observe people but how to listen with my eyes. How to stop listening to them talking and start observing them, then you can truly see who they are and what they want. Another significant influence was the quintessential Gestaltist Jim Simkin, who always left me marveling at how he did what he did. Where he could take clients and how he took them there was craftsman-like. I was also influenced by Michael Conant and his training in bioenergetics: how to understand the psyche of a person by looking at their body. How the bits fit together, the body holding patterns, where it bends and where it does not, and how it moves. I have never been interested in practicing body therapies but "body reading," as they call it, is a major part of bioenergetics, which again taught me how to observe people.

Then, of course, there is the theory of transactional analysis, of which cognitive behavior therapy forms a significant part. This provided me with the nuts and bolts and the practicalities of the counseling process, the behavioral things you do with the client.

I was recently asked by a supervisee what approach I use and I could not answer the question. I used to be able to answer, and was surprised that I felt I no longer could do so. I felt I could no longer satisfactorily identify an approach that would define me as a counselor or psychotherapist. Initially this concerned me, as it seemed a retrograde step. I had gone from knowing who I was to not knowing who I was. Needless to say I subsequently pondered this question for some time.

I can state the practicalities of what I do with a client and I can cite the influences on myself as a counselor, as I have done above. Perhaps that means I am now eclectic in my approach. I have never liked the idea of being an eclectic counselor, as it seems to be a collection of a lot of things but not really any of them. It seems to lack substance.

As I thought about the question in subsequent days, I wondered what had changed, so that a question I once could answer, I no longer could. In my musing I calculated that I would have done between 40,000 and 50,000 hours of counseling in my 32 years of working. It seems logical that if one does a task for that long, it stops being something that you do and becomes part of who you are. You have done the task so many times it becomes second nature, "in your bones," and part of your character.

This idea then allowed me to answer the question. I am a person, Tony White, and there are many parts or aspects of me, one being a counselor. When I go to work I am simply being me. This is what the client gets, me the person, with the counselor being part of me. I think I have shifted from being a counselor, who happens to be named Tony, to being Tony, who also happens to be a counselor. I now have some kind of answer should I be asked that question again. A two-tiered answer, the theoretical approach I use with the practicalities of counseling and a more deeper understanding of myself as a counselor as being part of my perception of who I am.

There are many others who have played a significant role in my professional life at some point. In the very early days there were people like Judy Pitt, with whom I ran my very first therapy groups, Sally Robinson, Lesley Rogers, Jan Coleman, Sister Columba, Robin Maslen, Paddy Glasgow, Meredyth Blackwell-Bell, Kate Meredith, Linda Gregory, Helen Gee, June Nielsen, and Julia Soloman, who showed me how to work with children. The Singapore connection, where I did many workshops, was also established in the early years and included people such as Jessica Leong, Irene Yong, Cheryl Leong, Eugene Fernandez, Betty Lim, and Paul Tan. Sydney on the east coast of Australia included others in the early days like Jan

Grant, Gail Broady, Libby Crichton, Enid Ware, Reiner and Di Schmidt, and Helen Rutherford.

In more recent years there has been Judy Morris, my sister Pippa White, Cliff Lockley, Sally Langsford, Nada Ilian, Mary-Anne Stewart, Ken Abrahams, Madeleine Hicks, Michelle French, Linda de Haan, and my introduction to drug counseling by Sue Helfgott, Louise Fletcher, Lauren Fricker, and Lyn Annandale. In more recent times my travel to Europe began in Croatia with Tatjana Gjurkovic and Jelena Vrsaljko, and then Serbia with Zoran Milivojevic, Natasa Djurica, who did many translations, Mirko Mitrovic, Milica Jankovic, who was the delightful translator at my workshops, Milena Stosic, Danijela Stojanovic, AlekSandra Bubera, Maja Stoparic, Tatjana Majer Banjac and Natasha Cvejic-Starcevic. Finally, with the completion of my masters degree, there has been Adrienne Lee, Ian Stewart, Mark Widdowson, and Boris Lee.

There have been many, many others who I apologize for not including. The final group who should always receive the highest appreciation are my clients over the years: the courageous people who have shown me great strength, trust, and the powerful will of the human being. Thank you so much for keeping my faith in human nature.

Introduction

Structure of the book

This book is divided into two parts. Part 1 presents an overview of alcohol and drugs in society, the various theories of addiction, and the fundamental components of counseling that form the foundations upon which the rest of the book is based. It also presents the theory of transactional analysis, as that is the main theory used in this book. Humans have always had drugs of some kind. Interestingly enough even animals will eat fermented fruit fallen from trees and experience drunkenness. However, regardless of our forefathers, humans have always used drugs and alcohol. They have been in every human society that ever existed on earth. This part of the book endeavors to articulate an overview of humans, their drug use, addiction and counseling.

Part 2 of the book builds on the foundations laid in Part 1 by explaining the specific techniques involved in counseling the drug and alcohol user. This includes such areas as harm reduction, motivational interviewing and assessment of the drug user. While Part 1 speaks in fairly general terms, Part 2 gets to the specific nuts and bolts of drug and alcohol counseling. In addition to this, much as about the teenage drug user. This is because teenagers are psychologically different to the fully grown adult, and in drug counseling one is often counseling adolescents or members of their family. In summary, Part 2 provides us with the micro-counseling skills required by the drug and alcohol counselor.

Terminology used in the book

In the addictions field there are many different ways one can refer to drugs and alcohol. Of course, alcohol is a drug and thus when one refers to drugs one is also technically referring to alcohol as well. However, in common parlance the man in the street tends to see the term "drugs" as referring to illegal drugs such as marijuana or cocaine and not the other drugs like alcohol, tobacco, and even caffeine, consumed via such things as coffee and cola drinks.

In this book, however, a reference to drugs usually means I am referring to alcohol as well, unless otherwise stated. Sometimes the terminology "alcohol and drugs" is used. This is common in the addictions literature. Along with drugs in general, alcohol gets specific mention because it is by far the most widely used and abused drug of all.

About the author

There is one question each drug and alcohol counselor fears and it can be asked at any time, by the client, who directly asks the counselor: "Do you now, or have you ever, used drugs?" By this question they are usually referring to illegal drugs or perhaps some kind of habitual drug use. Those who have used such drugs in the past may feel uncomfortable saying so, as they are advocating the client does not use drugs and that may seem a bit hypocritical. Those counselors who have not used drugs may not like revealing this because they think the client may lose some confidence in their ability to counsel drug users. They may feel the client sees them as ignorant about drugs and their use.

I have been asked this question only a few times over the past 25 years, so it is an uncommon occurrence, but it does happen. However, it seems reasonable to assume that most clients would ponder the question at some point, especially if a significant therapeutic relationship should develop between the client and therapist.

There are two schools of thought on how to respond to the question. Some respond by saying the question is irrelevant to the counseling and do not answer it. To my mind this is not a productive response, as it simply builds intrigue and leaves the client wondering why the counselor won't answer. It becomes a distraction and some clients may think it is not right that the counselor does not answer the question when they themselves are being asked many questions which they are meant to respond to.

The other school of thought prefers to answer the question, which, if asked, I do. I smoked cigarettes from my mid teens to early twenties. I gave up and restarted again a few times but eventually stopped completely and have not smoked since. At the time of writing this I am 54 years old. I dislike the taste of coffee, which I only consume very infrequently. From my mid teens to mid twenties I used both marijuana and LSD, at times heavily. I eventually felt I wanted more out of life and taking such drugs became boring. I slowly drifted out of the drug subculture and have never been back. I have used alcohol recreationally from my mid teen years and still do. If readers were wondering about the drug and alcohol use history of a person who would write a book about drugs and alcohol, it is now out in the open, so it seems we can get back to the topic at hand.

Professionally I began working as a counselor in private practice in my early twenties. Since then people have kept wanting to seek my counsel, so I have kept working in that way. In doing general counseling one meets many clients with alcohol and drug issues, so I learnt a lot about this from the very beginning of my professional career. About 20 years ago I did specialist training in addiction studies, as it was called then, and worked on a sessional basis in a drug rehabilitation center for five years. Obviously, during that time I learnt a great deal about drugs and drug users. I worked for three years in a prison and in that prison population many had extensive drug use histories. As many in the prison were on methadone treatment, I learnt a good deal about the psychology of the methadone user, how it works, how people respond to it in different ways, and how difficult it is to get off.

I worked for seven years with an organization that assisted the chronically mentally ill, mainly with schizophrenia, bipolar disorder, borderline personality disorder and psychotic depression. Major mental illness and drug use almost go hand in hand and again I found myself working with a population who had extensive alcohol and drug-use patterns. With this group I also learnt a good deal about mood-altering prescription medications and how they are used and abused: how they were obtained and consumed, how they are used in the drug subculture to trade or sell, so as to obtain other drugs, and so forth.

Conclusion

This book represents a statement about drugs and the drug users I have met over the past 30 years, in a variety of settings, as I have just described. Over that time I have developed some of my own ideas and therapeutic techniques. Many books on counseling drug and alcohol users are just "picture straightening." They reproduce the same material in different ways or from different perspectives— which is useful. However, I present some new ideas in this book, which I hope adds to the literature on the topic.

Part 1

Foundations of Drug and Alcohol Counseling

Chapter 1

Drugs and Addiction in Society

The Fundamentals

Introduction

The goal of this chapter is to provide an overview of drugs and drug counseling, including a look at the various concepts of addiction.

- The Australian Psychological Society (2005) note a long history of drug use in societies from all over the world.

- Alcohol use dates back at least 8000 years.

- Tobacco has been used for many hundreds of years, probably originating in the Americas before being taken to Europe.

- Evidence has shown that opium was used in Mesopotamia at least 7000 years ago.

- Archeologists in northern Europe found remnants of cannabis dating back to the fifth century BC.

- Hallucinogenic drugs have been very widely used throughout history, dating back at least 7500 years.

Mood-altering drugs are not new or abnormal in human society. The Australian Psychological Society (2005, p.36) states, "Substance use has always been and continues to be a part of ordinary human behavior." Indeed drugs can become an integral part of a society. If historically a particular drug has been used, then over time that drug and its use can become embedded in the culture. Indeed, often the drug use becomes part of the cultural identity. In Australia, having a beer around a barbecue with family and friends is part of the Australian cultural identity. Smoking long thin cigarettes in some European societies is viewed as a sophisticated thing for women to do and it becomes part of the way that culture views itself. Opium smoking was popular in Chinese culture for many years and it also became part of that cultural identity. Drug use allow cultures to define, in part, who they are.

Addiction

As a consequence it seems that drug and alcohol counseling are always going to be needed, as people seek not to lose control of their consumption. It is this that is the core part of the drug use question. Most people do not lose control of their drug and alcohol consumption. However, there is a group in every society who do and it is these who become the dependent drug users. While this group is but one small subset of all drug users, it is the one that takes up most of the resources, such as drug and alcohol counseling centers and health facilities required to cope with the physical problems dependent drug use brings with it.

In order to treat and help the ever-present dependent drug user in society different definitions or understandings of addiction and dependence have been formulated over time. It seems opportune to provide a brief review of them here, modified from Helfgott and Allsop (1997).

1. *Moral view of addiction.* This developed around the mid-nineteenth century. It takes the view that some people are considered unable to control their drug use and drinking because they have a moral weakness, a disease of the will, lack a spiritual conviction, or are bereft of faith or a belief in God. In this approach the problem is seen to exist inside the person. In most modern democracies around the world this is not currently a prominent view but it does still exist, mainly in certain religious groups.

2. *Pharmacological view of addiction.* Over time there was a shift in thinking to where addiction was seen to reside in the substance rather than in the individual, as is the case in the moral view. It was not so much about a weak individual, more about a powerful substance. This view came from the rise of temperance movements that existed around the early 1900s in countries like the UK, Australia, and the USA. The solution to addiction in this view is to remove the alcohol or drug from people so they cannot get addicted. The most infamous example of this was the Prohibition era in the USA.

3. *The disease view of addiction.* Subsequently there was a shift away from the prohibition of alcohol and drugs, and the disease view emerged. Again the problem was seen to exist inside the person, not external to them. In this case, the addiction to drugs is seen as a state of sickness that is beyond the control of the person. There is something physically wrong with the person. It may be a faulty genetic structure or a chemical imbalance in the brain.

   This is the medical model explanation of addiction. This is a strongly held view around the world at this time and represents the classical approach to psychiatry. The solution here is abstinence and to provide drugs that correct any chemical imbalances in the individual.

4. *Social learning view of addiction.* This emerged in the late 1960s. The model does not assert that people are morally bereft, mentally ill, or sick and powerless in the face of an overwhelming substance. Rather, it focuses on the interaction between the environment, the individual, and the drug as a way to understand addiction. It works in two ways.

   First, drug use is a learned behavior which may be learned from parents, peers, partners, and so forth. It is learned from observing others' use and the consequences of their own use.

   Second, drug use is functional. The consequences of using the drug are functional for the person. This may include feeling relaxed, high, sociable, and so forth. This view is currently widely held around the world.

5. *The psychodynamic and psychotherapeutic view of addiction.* This is a huge area that began to develop over a hundred years ago with Freud and psychoanalysis and is still widely used around the world. In this view, the problem is seen to reside within the individual, who is seen to be ill in psychological terms, unlike the disease model which sees the illness in physical terms.

   Since Freud this view has proliferated, with many new approaches appearing that are consistent with this approach to addiction. Two prominent ones are the Gestalt approach to addiction which began in the 1960s and the client-centered or Rogerian approach which developed in the 1950s. Both these are very widely used around the world today. In most

LIVERPOOL JOHN MOORES UNIVERSITY
LEARNING SERVICES

of these approaches the psychological illness is seen to result from some kind of adverse parenting the person received in childhood. Treatment involves regressing the client in some way, so as to remediate the early adverse experiences, and to use the therapeutic relationship between the client and therapist as an agent of change.

Transactional analysis

Transactional analysis is another prominent psychodynamic approach. It also evolved in the 1960s and is still a widely used approach to addiction, especially in Europe. This book has a transactional analysis approach and a transactional analysis theory of addiction is explained in detail in Chapter 3. However, whilst I am by no means a Gestalt therapist, I do use some of the techniques from that approach, as will become apparent, especially in the chapters on motivational interviewing and drug use ambivalence. It is probably most accurate to say that this book has a transactional analysis and Gestalt approach to addiction and drug counseling.

One of the main features of the transactional analysis approach is its ability to explain concepts in an easy and user-friendly way. As will be seen in this book there are many diagrams, which are central to the transactional analysis approach. The beauty of this is that clients can easily come to understand why they have problems with addiction by simply viewing such diagrams, such as their drug use ambivalence. The first step in any counseling approach is awareness and transactional analysis is the most effective way of raising client awareness about their difficulties.

Drugs are a political issue

Unfortunately drugs are a political issue and this causes difficulties for the drug counselor in a number of ways. I discuss some of these in more detail in the next chapter, and they include ideas like drug-induced psychosis, gateway drugs, and information on the effects of drugs. The topic of drugs can be an emotional issue for some which brings out a diversity of strong views about drugs and drug use. There is a variety of groups in most communities that have quite divergent views about drugs. These can include various religious groups, temperance movements, and pro-legalization of drugs groups. Different governments have differing political positions on the legality or illegality of drugs.

This causes problems for the drug counselor because it makes it harder to get accurate information about drugs, as the various groups will present the "facts" of drugs in a way that supports their political agenda. This has been mentioned in other textbooks on drug counseling, for instance by Marsh and Dale (2006). They state that, "Contrary to popular belief, most people who use substances do so in ways that cause them relatively little harm. Their use does not interfere significantly in their lives or the lives of others in terms of negative consequences" (p.13).

They are pointing out that a significant group of people are misinformed about the negative effects of drugs and of course some of those will be drug counselors. It seems obvious that drug counselors must have a correct understanding of the effects of drugs, but this is more difficult to achieve than one would think. Drug and alcohol counselors need to be aware of who is providing information about drugs, when reading it, and what their political position is on drugs. As mentioned above, more will be said about this in the next chapter.

Conclusion

This chapter provided an introduction to and overview of the area of drugs, drug use, and the counseling of drug users. It included the following points:

Drugs and alcohol have been used in almost every society for many thousands of years.

The five main different views of addiction were presented and included the moral view, the pharmacological view, the disease view, the social learning view, and the psychodynamic view. These differing views have resulted in alternative methods of dealing with drugs in society and the specifics of counseling drug and alcohol users.

A brief overview of the contribution of transactional analysis to drug and alcohol counseling was explained and also how Gestalt psychology will is used in this book to enhance the transactional analysis approach.

Finally, the emergence of drugs as a political issue and the problems this causes for the drug counselor, most notably difficulties in obtaining accurate information on the effects and hazards of various drugs, are discussed.

Chapter 2

Fundamental Components of Drug Counseling

The facts about drugs

People who seek counseling about drugs, including the drug user and significant others (close relatives and loved ones), often require this type of information. This chapter will provide a variety of information that the drug counselor needs to be aware of when counseling. It begins with an overview of the different types of drugs, the peak ages of use, and how the concept of gateway drugs shows possible interactions between them. This is logically followed by a discussion of the idea of drug of choice and polydrug use. Finally the three important areas of informing clients fully about the effects of drugs, random urine testing, and drug-induced psychosis are covered.

Main groups of drugs

There are many kinds of drugs but the drugs discussed in this book are psychoactive drugs. A psychoactive drug is any drug that affects the central nervous system (CNS) and can produce mood changes or distorted perception.

There are three main types:

Depressants

Depressants decrease alertness by slowing down the activity of the CNS. They are called depressants because they slow down the heart rate and breathing and can also cause reduced concentration and coordination. One of the main problems with depressants is they can lead to a fatal overdose. This is especially so when depressant drugs are used together, such as heroin with alcohol.

Depressant drugs include:

- alcohol

- marijuana (also a hallucinogen)

- opioids such as heroin, morphine, pethidine, methadone, and codeine

- barbiturates like Tuinal, Amytal, and Seconal

- some inhalants and solvents

- benzodiazepines like Valium, Mogadon, Rohypnol, and Serapax

- GBH or fantasy.

Stimulants

Stimulants increase the body's level of arousal by increasing the activity in the brain. The CNS is speeded up. This tends to result in an increase in heart rate, body temperature, concentration, alertness, and feelings of confidence.

Stimulant drugs include:

- nicotine in tobacco

- caffeine in coffee, tea, and some cola drinks

- medicines like cold and flu tablets, which contain pseudoephedrine

- dexamphetamine and Ritalin, which are used to treat conditions like attention-deficit hyperactivity disorder (ADHD)

- amphetamines, both prescribed and illegal (e.g. ice, crystal meth, and speed)

- cocaine

- ecstasy (also a hallucinogen).

Hallucinogens

The third group are the hallucinogens which can cause a change in a person's thought, emotion, perception, and consciousness. Unlike stimulants, which merely amplify familiar states of mind, these cause experiences that are different from normal consciousness. People may see or hear things that are not there or are distorted in some way. In essence, hallucinations of various kinds and in varying degrees are experienced. This can lead to positive effects of euphoria or negative effects of panic, paranoia, and confusion.

Hallucinogenic drugs include:

- LSD
- PCP or angel dust
- magic mushrooms
- mescaline
- marijuana (also a depressant)
- ecstasy (also a stimulant).

Peak ages of use and other drug user features

The following data comes from the American Psychiatric Association (1994), which provides important data about the various categories of drugs and how they are used. Of particular note is the end point of the peak age of drug use. People tend to grow out of habitual and recreational drug use. This is important when counseling the dependent type of drug user who is commonly know as the "drug addict." These people find it very hard to stop and one can therefore adopt the treatment approach of management, getting them through to that age where they start to grow out of the use. More will be said about this in a later chapter.

In addition, if a user does not fit the usual pattern described, that may mean they have some unusual personality features. This can be useful in treatment planning, because if they do not fit the usual pattern this can at times be used to assist in their counseling.

Amphetamines

Peak age of use is 18 to 30 years. Those who develop a dependency are not likely to last longer than 8 to 10 years of use, as unpleasant side effects can occur which make the drug less attractive. When the drug is smoked or taken intravenously dependence tends to occur more quickly than if it is taken orally. There tend to be two patterns of use that develop: chronic daily use, where there are no wide variations in the dose being used. However, over time there tends to be an increase in the dose used. The second pattern is episodic use where the person stops using for a number of days and then may binge, over the weekend for example.

Caffeine

Peak age of use is 20 to 65 years.

Cannabis

Peak age of use is 18 to 30 years. If a person is going to experiment with illicit drugs cannabis is often tried first, usually in the teenage years. It is often taken with other drugs, such as alcohol or cocaine. Dependence usually develops over a long period of time where the dependent user establishes a pattern of chronic use with a gradual increase in the frequency and amount used.

Cocaine

Peak age of use is 18 to 30 years. It is similar to amphetamines, with two types of use developing over time: daily chronic use and episodic bingeing use. In addition, dependence is more rapid when it is taken intravenously or smoked. "Snorting" involves a slower progression to dependence, usually over months or years. Cocaine is usually expensive, so its use can be governed by the availability of money or dependent users may resort to criminal activities to get a regular supply.

Hallucinogens

Peak age of use is 26 to 34 years. Many users stop as they get older, unlike alcohol and tobacco. Flashbacks are reported by some users, which sometimes cause distress, though to others they are not distressing. The younger the user the greater the tendency for unpleasant experiences and males are three times more likely to use than females.

Inhalants

Peak age of use is in adolescence. The easy availability of inhalants tend to make them the drug of choice for younger people. Some begin as young as nine years of age and they are much less commonly used by those in their thirties. With most inhalants the onset of intoxication is rapid and peaks after a few minutes. Dependent users can use repeatedly throughout the day to maintain the intoxication. There are numerous medical problems that can result from persistent inhalant use.

Nicotine

First age of use can be in the early teens and then the course of use varies significantly, ranging from a brief period of use to a lifetime of chronic use. As with inhalants, nicotine is one of the more physically dangerous drugs with many potential medical conditions developing because of ongoing use.

Opioids

Peak age of use is 20 to 40 years. Dependence can occur at any age but is more likely if it shows up first in the late teens or early twenties. Once a significant dependence develops it tends to last over years. During that time there are often many brief periods of abstinence with relapse following reasonably quickly. The difficulty for the opioid dependent person is not getting off the drug but staying off the drug.

These are some common features of use for the different types of drugs. However, one must remember that these refer mainly to problem drug use. The majority of drug users suffer few ill effects from using drugs. As a drug counselor, one needs to keep this in mind, in particular when dealing with younger drug users or significant others who worry about the drug use of their loved one. There can be a lot of unnecessary anxiety, as most never develop a drug use problem.

Gateway drugs

One of the common concerns of parents for their child who is discovered using drugs is that this is their first step in a lifelong battle with drug addiction. For instance, the mother who finds a marijuana cigarette in her 15-year-old daughter's room thinks this is going to result in a lifelong heroin addiction for her. This is not uncommonly presented to drug counselors and refers to the idea of gateway drugs: drugs that are seen to act as a gateway to other drug taking, such as the fear that marijuana will lead to heroin use.

In such counseling one can begin by quoting worried parents some statistics. The Australian Institute of Health and Welfare (2007) notes that the highest age group having ever used marijuana and heroin is 30–39-year-olds. (Most modern democracies would have similar statistics.)

- 30–39-year-olds—54.6 percent have used marijuana

- 30–39-year-olds—2.7 percent have used heroin.

These statistics clearly show that the vast majority of marijuana users do not go on to use heroin: 54.6 percent of that age group have smoked marijuana, while only 2.7 percent have used heroin. Indeed many, if not most, of those 2.7 percent would also have been recreational users and never developed any serious dependency on the drug. The dependent heroin user comprises only a very small group of people. However, they get lots of press because their lives are often filled with angst and excitement, which makes for a good story, as seen in movies and on television.

The idea of one drug leading to the use of other drugs has been about for many years. Very few people begin their first drug use with heroin or methamphetamine. Those who progress further with drugs typically begin with alcohol and cigarettes, which may then be followed by marijuana and then other illicit drugs (Kandel and Faust 1975). It has been noted that problem drinking can sometimes lead to a pattern of ongoing marijuana use, sometimes with other illicit drugs. The age of first use is one of the more important factors in predicting the subsequent use of other drugs (Kandel and Faust 1975). The younger the age of first use of alcohol or marijuana the more likely there will be subsequent use of other drugs.

However, one needs to keep all this in context. Over the years I have counseled many fathers and mothers who have come to me distressed about their adolescent child. Mother may have "inadvertently" stumbled across a marijuana joint secreted in her daughter's bedroom whilst cleaning it. On the odd occasion they will even produce it in the session for me to see!

My response is to provide the context of the statistics and the fact that many teenagers will experiment a few times with marijuana (and other drugs), find it is not for them, and rarely use it again. Peer pressure can work for a time, but if the adolescent finds the drug does nothing for them or makes them feel worse they will cease the use and if necessary will move to a new peer group. Many teenage peer groups are comprised of some who do smoke marijuana and drink and some who do not. However, there is a small group for whom alcohol and marijuana do act as a gateway to subsequent problematic drug use. I recommend the parents talk with the teenager or even get the teenager to see a counselor so it can be brought into the open and then deal with what needs to be dealt with.

Finally, it should be noted, as mentioned in Chapter 1, that drugs and politics become intertwined in the area of gateway drugs. Some groups who have an anti-drug view have used the idea of marijuana being a gateway drug as a rationale for the continued prohibition of that drug (Lynskey, Vink, and Boomsma (2006). As I said in Chapter 1, this is unfortunate, as it simply complicates matters in finding out the actual facts about marijuana's possible role as a gateway drug. Debate continues on the topic of gateway drugs and parents need to be counseled about the politicization of drugs by both sides on this matter.

Drug of choice

Related to the idea of gateway drugs is the notion of "drug of choice." Most drug users can define the drug they prefer most, which can be shown by the following equation:

drug of choice = physiology + psychology

The preferred drug will be the result of the person's physiological reaction to the drug and what the drug provides for them psychologically. A client recently stated: "Amphetamines were my preferred drugs. They were the drugs that I would go looking for. If other drugs were there like marijuana or alcohol I would take them but I would not go looking for them." This is probably quite a good way to define a drug of choice. That special drug will motivate the user to search for it, whereas others drugs will not. To become the drug of choice, first it must work for the person physiologically. Sometimes a particular drug and a person's physiology just do not fit. Below are a few comments which reflect this.

A 30-year-old woman talks about her alcohol use: "I can only drink three nights a week. If I drink any more I just start to feel sick." It is highly unlikely she will ever develop a drinking problem because physically her body cannot take anymore than two or three nights drinking per week.

A 25-year-old woman discusses her brief history with marijuana: "I tried marijuana about a dozen times but all it did was make me fall asleep. What is the point of taking a so-called social drug, if you fall asleep." She will never become a habitual marijuana user because physiologically the drug does not work for her.

A 20-year-old male describes his reaction to heroin: "I injected heroin a few times but each time I did I threw up." Again it is highly unlikely he will ever develop a heroin addiction, not because of any psychological reason but because heroin and his physiology do not fit.

Finally we have the example of Antabuse. When a person takes Antabuse and then drinks alcohol it causes some most unpleasant physical reactions, such as vomiting, flushing of the skin, and a bad headache. For these reasons it is sometimes used to treat alcoholism. However, Craighead and Nemeroff (2004, p.65) note, "For genetic reasons, some people produce lower than average amounts of the enzyme aldehyde dehydrogenase. Drinking alcohol produces for them symptoms similar to, although generally milder than, those associated with Antabuse. About half of Chinese and Japanese people have low amounts of this enzyme, and partly because of this lack, alcohol abuse has historically been less common in China and Japan than in most other countries."

Genetics and the resultant physiological makeup are a most important factor in the development (or lack) of a drug problem and a person's drug of choice. However, the other half of the equation is the psychology. One may have a positive physical reaction to a drug but it will only become attractive if the person's psychology is right. This has long been noted in problem drug users who self-medicate. The user discovers that the drug allows them to medicate a psychological problem away. If they have symptoms of attention-deficit disorder (ADD) they may find that marijuana allows them to focus more or if they suffer depression they may find that alcohol stops the depression for a while. Besides these problem drug users, all recreational drug users are of a similar vein. Their psychology must be right for a drug to become attractive and indeed usable at all. Identifying a person's drug of choice can provide some good diagnostic insights into their psychological makeup.

Consider these comments:

- "I never liked drinking because it made me feel out of control"—indicating a psychological need to have a sense of control.

- "When I smoked marijuana I used to get really paranoid"—indicating possible paranoid personality features in the user.

- "I like cocaine because of the clarity it gives me. I like clarity and focus in my life"—drug provides a personality feature desired by the user.

- "I started to take heroin and it made me go to sleep for the next ten years"—drug provides a desired personality feature, to withdraw from life by sleeping.

The first two examples show how the person's psychology will hinder any drug use problem developing and the last two show how the psychology could allow a drug problem to develop. These examples also show how the psychology of a person effects the drug of choice for the recreational drug user. Those who never develop a drug dependency are going to have a drug of choice that suits their psychology in some way as well. As a result, isolating the person's drug of choice can assist the counselor in understanding the psychology of the client.

Polydrug use

Anyone in the drug counseling field will come across the term polydrug use. This is seen as the contrary of monodrug use. In real terms there are very few monodrug users at all. The vast majority of people are polydrug users. If someone has a glass of wine during dinner and a cup of coffee at the end they are a polydrug user, using both alcohol and the stimulant caffeine. However, the term polydrug use usually refers to the use of illicit drugs, maybe with alcohol, in one drug-taking session. The person ingests a combination of drugs in the one session.

Where polydrug use assumes most importance is when considering the possibility of drug overdose. The drug counselor needs to be cognizant of the possible effects of a combinations of drugs. Overdose from one single drug is much less common that overdose from multiple drug consumption. One study of drug-related overdose, Hickman *et al.* (2006), found only one drug present in just 11 percent of deaths, with the average number being more than three drugs detected in the deceased. The most common drugs found in overdose were heroin, cocaine, benzodiazepines, alcohol, and methadone. The least common were amphetamines, ecstasy, and cannabis (also see Giroud *et al.* 1997; McKenna 2002; and Newcombe and Wood, in White 2011).

As a matter of course any drug counselor will enquire as to what drugs the client is using. They should specifically ask if the person uses heroin, cocaine, benzodiazepines, alcohol, and/or methadone and in what combinations in any one drug-taking session. If there is a combination then the counselor would obviously inform the client of the potential for overdose and look at ways by which the client can reduce the risk of a fatal overdose, such as by not using alone and so forth.

The need to be truthful with clients

This is a difficult area indeed for the drug counselor. When running workshops on drug counseling this is one area where I often come under fire from some of the participants. It generates strong emotional responses for some and it relates to the dangers of drugs. It seems reasonable to conclude that a counselor needs to be fully honest with clients about drugs and their dangers.

From my own personal experience of talking to drug counselors, listening to them in workshops, and reading articles they write, there is a tendency by many, if not most, to exaggerate the dangers of drugs to clients. The motive for this has the client's best interest at heart and the thinking of the counselor is often something like, "If I can scare the person about the effects of drugs then they will be less inclined to use." They are using the scare tactics approach in an endeavor to help prevent the client from using drugs. While one can understand this, it can and does damage the relationship with the client when they realize they are not being told the full truth.

For example, take the case of ecstasy. In the literature one quickly finds lists of the effects and dangers of ecstasy, as in: Drug and Alcohol Office (2006); Government of Western Australia—Drug and Alcohol Office (2008); McGill (2006). These lists contain statements about the effects of ecstasy and the dangers of ecstasy. Readers are told that it is possible to overdose on ecstasy, that it can cause depression and psychosis, the risks of overheating and dehydration, and how ecstasy tablets almost always have other unknown ingredients in them. These are all true but it is not the whole truth.

They are not told what Marsh and Dale (2006) say, that most people who use substances do so in ways that cause them relatively little harm. Of all the drugs, including alcohol and tobacco, it is ecstasy, LSD, and marijuana that are the safest. There is significant research to support this, including Newcombe and Woods (in White 2011), who rate ecstasy as "Quite low risk," and Nutt *et al.* (2007), who show that ecstasy is one of the least harmful drugs of all.

This leaves the drug counselor in a difficult position. I am not for a moment suggesting that one makes loud public statements highlighting the relative safety of taking ecstasy. What I am saying is that the counselor has to tell the drug user the truth and the whole truth about the dangers of drugs when necessary. Regarding ecstasy, at the very least one would need to say that there is a significant body of evidence which indicates it is one of the safer drugs going around.

By the time they get to counseling, most clients have heard all about the dangers of drugs from parents, the police, health officials, teachers, and so forth. Things like: marijuana is dangerous because it makes you go crazy and it is the first gateway drug to a lifetime of drug addiction. This incongruence is eloquently stated by a young English boy cited in Pickering (1972):

> The following article was written by a sixteen-year-old English boy and appeared in his local parish magazine.
>
> When you first arrive at Tangier in Morocco, you recoil with horror when you are approached by young men trying to sell you marihuana or hashish or whatever you like to call it (in Morocco it is universally called "kif"). You have thoughts of glassy-eyed junkies wasting away in dens full of drug addicts. After a few days or a few weeks (or never at all with some people) you begin to get a different impression—you find that most of the people you know smoke or have smoked it, and those who have are not one jot different from those who have never touched it. (p.298)

After this personal discovery in the real world what will this young English boy conclude? He trusted those who told him that smoking marijuana would result in him becoming a glassy-eyed junkie wasting away in a den full of drug addicts. He will begin to realize that his trust has been broken. As any counselor will tell you, one of the most important things in counseling is the therapeutic relationship. Trust, of course, is at the core of such an important relationship, which means you have to be trustworthy in the information which you give to the client. You have to tell them the truth and the whole truth because, like the young English boy, sooner or later they will discover the real-world truth for themselves with their own observations. As I mentioned above, most clients will be expecting you to exaggerate some of the dangers to them and when you do not they will be surprised, which can only enhance the therapeutic relationship.

Urine testing

With the increase in random urine testing for drugs an ever-increasing number of clients bring this issue to counseling. Most want to discuss ways to get around the testing, usually how long before testing do they have to stop using, and the possibility of masking agents. There have been a lot of possible masking agents put forth by clients over the years and many rumors and myths about them. Some are clearly nonsense and others are unreliable at best, such as drinking large amounts of water before the test, so that the drug in the urine is significantly diluted to avoid detection. Some shops that sell drug paraphernalia will also sell apparent masking agents. I have never heard of what I would judge to be a reliable masking agent, much to the dismay of many drug-using clients. However, as the number of people being urine tested grows it is quite possible that in the future it will become economic to produce and sell reliable masking agents for recreational drugs.

Whilst working in prison I was once shown a device found on a prisoner. It was a small hard plastic balloon with a thin plastic tube coming out of it. The balloon was held between the buttocks and the tube would run out underneath the penis. When the buttocks were squeezed together liquid would come out of the end of the plastic tubing giving the indication that urine was being passed. This demonstrates that the desire and ingenuity to try and bypass urine drug testing is considerable. Drug counselors also need to be cognizant of the time it takes for a "clean urine," as they call it. It should be noted that drugs can also be detected by the analysis of hair, blood, sweat, and saliva, but urine testing is the most common.

Below is a rough guide to how long it takes to give a clean urine. Of course it depends on a variety of factors such as the purity of the drug taken, how much was taken, the metabolism of the person, their age, and so forth. This comes from the Western Australian Drug Users and AIDS Association, Inc.

Table 2.1 Time for clearance of drugs from urine

Drug	Clearance time
Amphetamine	2–4 days
Ecstasy	2–4 days
Cannabis	casual use 2–7 days
	heavy use up to 30 days
Alcohol	12–24 hours
Valium	1–2 days
Heroin	1–2 days
Cocaine	12 hrs–3 days
Methadone	2 days
LSD	2–3 days

Paruresis

Whilst on the topic of urine testing, the drug counselor also needs to be aware of a condition known as paruresis. This was brought to my attention when I worked in the prison system as a psychologist. Some inmates who were required to give a urine sample stated they could not do so because they could not urinate in public. When giving a urine sample one has to urinate in a cup as the tester watches. Indeed, they have to watch quite closely as the inmate could have some other container of liquid which they deposit in the cup. I was required to assess some inmates to see if they were truly paruretic or if they were falsely claiming to be so, so that they could avoid giving a sample on that occasion. It seems reasonable to conclude that as urine drug testing increases, drug-using clients are going to present the idea of paruresis more often. This group will consist of those who are truly paruretic and those who falsely claim to be.

As mentioned above, paruresis is the inability to urinate in public, including in public toilets. It is an anxiety-based condition that can range from mild levels of anxiety, which make urination difficult, to severe levels where urination is simply impossible and self-catheterization is required. Some common features of paruresis are:

- being anxious or unable to urinate in public

- worry that someone might knock on the toilet door or see or hear them urinate

- paruresis usually occurs when using public toilets

- it can occur at home when other people are in the house

- the difficulty disappears when the person is confident that no one else is around or likely to arrive

- they see urination in public as a type of performance and a "be perfect" frame of mind may be involved in this

- usually the only truly safe toilet is at home and this is often the only place where the paruretic can consistently urinate freely

- paruresis is often progressive in nature, where the fears of using public toilets grows over time and increasingly limits the person's movement outside the home

- severe paruetics can spend considerable amounts of time waiting for everyone to leave the public toilet before they urinate or they might completely avoid public toilets

- paruresis can start at any age and affects mainly boys and men, although girls and women can also suffer from it. While the research is limited, surveys suggest that up to 7 percent of the population are paruretic.

In working with a drug-using client who claims to be paruretic one would be asking questions which elicit this type of information. If he presents responses that are consistent with the above list of features, then he is either paruretic or has studied the features of paruresis. If his responses are inconsistent then it is possible the client is attempting to use this as a way to avoid such random urine tests. If the person is a severe paruretic, then it seems incumbent on the organization to use other types of drug testing such as blood testing.

Drug-induced psychosis

It is inevitable that any drug counselor will come across clients who report they have had a drug-induced psychosis (DIP). The client will be either self-diagnosed or a health professional will have given the diagnosis. This is a term one commonly finds in the drug counseling profession and it is the source of considerable debate in the literature (Tucker 2009). My personal view is that it is significantly overdiagnosed in counseling circles. This is a significant problem because any successful treatment must first begin with an accurate diagnosis.

I am unaware of any research on possible overdiagnosis of DIP, so instead this is based on my listening to clients talk, and, more importantly, talking with other drug counselors and mental health professionals. In my view there is a tendency to diagnose someone who displays psychotic symptoms and who has taken drugs like amphetamines and marijuana as having a DIP. At times there is little or no attempt to try and elicit whether the drugs actually induced the psychosis or not. In essence the *induced* part has been forgotten when the diagnosis is made. One of the reasons for this is that the diagnosis of a DIP is a difficult diagnosis to make with any certainty. The diagnostician must be certain that the hallucinations and/or delusions are the direct result of the drug ingested. This certainty can be compromised in a number of ways.

First, the information required to make such a determination usually comes from the individual himself and this person has possibly suffered a psychotic break of some kind. This means his ability to perceive reality, recall what happened, and to report some kind of time line of the drugs and psychotic symptoms has been significantly disrupted, often quite recently. That's what a psychosis is, a disruption in basic cognitive processing, which is what is required to provide reliable information. As a result the reliability of such information from the client is always questionable.

Second, the onset of psychotic symptoms is at times difficult to determine as they can evolve slowly over time, and some find that marijuana and alcohol may actually reduce some of the symptoms initially. Did the drugs come first or did the psychotic symptoms come first can be hard to decide with any certainty. For the diagnosis of a drug-induced psychosis the psychotic symptoms must not precede the beginning of the first ingestion of the drugs.

If the psychotic symptoms came first then it is not a DIP. The drugs may subsequently make matters worse but they did not induce the psychotic symptoms initially. Consider this case study.

***

CASE STUDY 2.1: *DRUG-INDUCED PSYCHOSIS?*

A 30-year-old woman with the diagnosis of schizophrenia reports she was formally diagnosed by a psychiatrist at 19 years of age and notes that on reflection the psychotic symptoms began developing around 14 or 15 years of age. This included hearing voices and paranoid delusions. She reports that it is like having a radio with all the stations on at the same time going on inside her head. She also reports that when she takes her antipsychotic medication the voices dramatically reduce in just a few days and the radio is switched off.

She recounts that she had a single marijuana cigarette when she was about 15 and a marijuana cookie when she was about 17 and that this was her only drug use at that time. She started smoking marijuana regularly when she was about 20. She had periods of using amphetamines regularly in her late twenties. She reports that when she smokes marijuana it can make the symptoms worse if she is in a down mood but it makes the symptoms less if she is in a good mood. She also reports that amphetamines have little or no effect on her schizophrenic symptoms.

In the last period she used amphetamines regularly for about 18 months. In this time she forgot to take her antipsychotic medication regularly and she attributes the increase in her symptoms to this. She has now not used for two months, her symptoms have reduced dramatically, and she copes quite well with life.

This case study shows some interesting features of this diagnosis. Many would diagnose this woman as having a DIP. Assuming her recollection is accurate, one has to determine a time line of events for the diagnosis of a DIP to be made, see Figure 2.1.

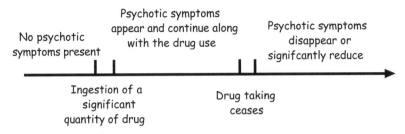

Figure 2.1 Drug-induced psychosis time line

Adapted from American Psychiatric Association (1994)

One must ascertain that there were no psychotic symptoms prior to the first ingestion of a significant amount of drugs. In Case study 2.1 the subject smoked only one marijuana cigarette, which would be very unlikely to precipitate a psychosis even though it was at age 15, about the same time she thinks the psychotic symptoms were developing. However, to determine with any certainty if symptoms were there before any drugs were taken is difficult, as often the symptoms develop slowly and the person is not really aware of what is happening, thus making the time line hard to ascertain. In addition the onset of a first psychotic episode not uncommonly occurs in the late teens or early twenties, the same age that people are often first experimenting with drug taking, so it could be pure coincidence that they occur around the same time.

Her next drug taking was eating a marijuana cookie at age 17. This decreases the probability of the diagnosis of a DIP as the symptoms continued to increase when there was no drug taking at all for two years and then very minimal drug taking (one marijuana cookie). As Figure 2.1 shows, the symptoms must continue whilst the drug taking continues and then stop or reduce when the drug taking ceases. She started her regular drug use at age 20, demonstrating the time line does not apply in this instance. She reports that recently she has stopped all drug use and her symptoms have diminished significantly, which does seem to fit with the end part of the time line. However, has the reduction been because she stopped using drugs or because now she is taking her antipsychotic medication properly? Another often difficult fact to ascertain, again demonstrating how hard it is to make the diagnosis of a DIP with any certainty.

As mentioned above, it is my view that this condition is currently overdiagnosed. However, in drug or any other type of counseling, one needs to obtain as clear and accurate a diagnosis as possible if any subsequent treatment to be successful. One must therefore be vigilant not to overdiagnose this when there are current pressures to do so. Often there can be significant pressure from parents or close loved ones for such a diagnosis. If such a diagnosis is made they can think, "He is not really schizophrenic. It's the drug that made him go crazy and so when he stops using he will be normal again." One can understand their desire for the diagnosis of a DIP but one must not succumb to such pressure and be as candid with them as one can.

The point at hand is that the counselor must be clear and open with clients about the situation of a DIP, including its tendency to be overdiagnosed. Not uncommonly one will be referred clients with such a diagnosis and one needs to take a closer look at the client to see if they do in fact follow the time line described in Figure 2.1. It also seems fair to suggest to clients that if there is any predisposition for psychosis then it is most unwise to use drugs like cannabis and amphetamines.

Conclusion

This chapter covered a number of areas that drug counselors will come across in their work. It provided basic information about drugs that provide a foundation for the underlying concepts for the micro-counseling techniques to be described later.

It included the following points:

- A description of the three main groups of drugs—depressants, stimulants, and hallucinogens—and how these affect the central nervous system and the effect that has on the body's arousal. Examples are given of various drugs in each category and some of the common brand names.

- A description of the peak ages of drug use for different drugs. This is seen as important information because it shows the ages when the dependent drug user may grow out of their drug use. It also highlights unusual clinical situations if the drug user is using a drug outside the peak ages of use, which is important in planning one's counseling approach.

- The concept of gateway drugs and the idea that alcohol and marijuana use will lead to more dangerous drug use with drugs such as heroin and amphetamines. While this does occur, it is only with a small number of drug users. Also presented are the predictive signs for the likely use of other, more addictive drugs in later life.

- The idea of the drug of choice having a physical and psychological component. The favored drug of the user will depend on the user having a suitable physiological makeup and suitable psychology for the drug.

- Polydrug use and its role in overdose. In the vast majority of cases a drug overdose is not the result of one drug but the result of a combination of a number of drugs. This chapter cites the most dangerous combinations of drugs that may lead to an overdose.

- The difficulty with getting reliable information about the effects of drugs and the need to be fully candid with clients. Some drug counselors attempt to use scare tactics with their clients in order to stop them using drugs such as marijuana and ecstasy. This at times involves exaggerating the dangers of some drugs and withholding other information about certain drugs, so as to give an unrealistically dangerous view of some drugs. The problem in doing this is eventually the client realizes the counselor is exaggerating the dangers and looses some trust in the counselor.

- The features of urine testing and paruresis. With the prevalence of urine testing for drugs increasing, the drug counselor needs to be aware of what is involved in the process of testing and other things like paruresis (the inability to urinate in public). Other information such as the time it takes since ingesting a drug before it becomes undetectable in urine and the possibility of masking agents also needs to be understood by the counselor and are covered in the chapter.

- The need to diagnose a drug-induced psychosis accurately and the difficulty in doing so. All drug counselors will come across clients who have been given the diagnosis of a drug-induced psychosis. This chapter explains exactly what a drug-induced psychosis is and the problems with its diagnosis.

Chapter 3

Transactional Analysis and the Theory of Addiction

This chapter will present two aspects of transactional analysis: first, some of the basic concepts, so that this book can be understood, and second the transactional analysis theory of addiction. Transactional analysis was developed by Eric Berne, who is most widely known for his 1964 book, *Games People Play*. It is a comprehensive theory of personality, human communication, relationships, and psychotherapy. This chapter provides an introduction to the theory so it can be used in counseling drug users. The concepts of ego states and transactions are presented here as these are necessary to understand the book. There is much more to the theory of transactional analysis, such as psychological games and life scripts. If you wish to get a deeper understanding of this theory it is recommended you read *TA Today* (Stewart and Joines 1987), which is a good overall introduction to the theory.

Theory of personality

Berne proposed three aspects of personality, which he called ego states: the Parent ego state, the Adult ego state and the Child ego state, which can be represented by three circles and labeled P, A, and C, as shown in Figure 3.1.

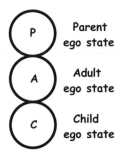

Figure 3.1 The three ego states of personality

Berne differentiated the Parent ego state, Adult ego state, and Child ego state from actual parents, adults, and children by using capital letters when describing them. (In this book when a capital is used it refers to an ego state rather than an actual, parent, adult or child.)

The Parent ego state

The Parent ego state is that part of the personality which represents the prominent figures in life who the person modeled herself on. It is a historical record of those who have made an impression on the individual such that they have been imitated. This usually includes people like mother and father, perhaps older siblings, significant peers, teachers, and so forth. The modeling into the Parent ego state continues for one's entire life from when a person born until she dies. For instance, spouses can copy and model each other, introjecting each others traits and behaviors. However, usually the most important and powerful modeling occurs in childhood, with the parents or parent-type figures being the principal models.

Such modeling is inevitable and will continue to happen whether one wants it or not. This is sometimes called the imitative instinct. People will instinctively copy others and are often quite unaware of it. The modeling is indiscriminate, as the child will model both healthy and unhealthy behaviors of the parents. If the child sees mother drinking alcohol, then she will model on that and it is stored in the Parent ego state, like a recording. The Parent ego state is a collection of recordings of various significant others and can be represented as shown in Figure 3.2.

Figure 3.2 shows the main modeling figures of the individual, and these modeled behaviors will tend to be displayed throughout her life. When the youngster grows up and has her own children sometimes she finds she is doing and saying things to her own children that were said to her as a child. She will tend to do this automatically and without even realizing it. If the parenting was healthy and constructive, then the child will model those behaviors. If the parenting was not healthy or growth promoting, then those behaviors will also be modeled.

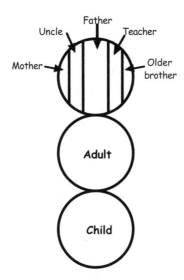

Figure 3.2 The Parent ego state as a set of recordings collected by the child

---

CASE STUDY 3.1: *BEHAVIOR MODELING*

A 30-year-old man who was doing a significant stretch of prison time for drug offences reports that as a child he lived on a farm. Besides having an orchard that required considerable work, his father also had a large underground hydroponic marijuana-growing operation for a number of years. Eventually they moved off the property and were never caught. The man reports how he would help his father work the orchard as well as tend the hydroponic marijuana-growing operation. He would work next to his father, maintaining the marijuana plants.

He reports the first paid job he ever had was given to him by his father. At the age of ten at harvesting time, his father would give him 50 cents for each sandwich bag full of marijuana that he would prepare and weigh correctly. He would work alongside his father, harvesting the crop in this way. They spent many hours working together like this.

This man, as a child, would have modeled this behavior and it would form one of the recordings in his Parent ego state. This is especially so as it occurred when he was young, happened many times, the modeling figure was his father, and it was an important way he had some "quality" time with his father. It becomes part of his personality whether he likes it or not. This does not mean he will display the same behavior, as he has other recordings in his Parent ego state and his Adult and Child ego states also have a strong determining influence on how he behaves. However, the Parent ego state recording is there in his personality, so he has more potential to show such behavior than someone who never modeled such things. As it turns out, in later life he did become involved in drug production and ended up in prison.

Besides these recordings, the Parent ego state also contains all the morals, values, and beliefs about what is good and bad behavior. These are also copied from parent-type figures in life. Thus the Parent ego state is important in that it makes us behave in a socialized way, if such behavior has been modeled, unlike Case study 3.1. Without the Parent ego state we would not have any guilt and thus could not have a stable society as anarchy would reign. It keeps the more primal urges found in the Child ego state in check. As a result, those who form the criminal population often have a dysfunctional Parent ego state, they are undersocialized and thus they commit crimes. It also works the other way as well. When the Parent ego state is too big the person becomes oversocialized and can develop things like anxiety and depression.

The Adult ego state

The Adult ego state represents that part of the personality that processes reality, makes decisions, and understands what is going on. Sometimes it is seen as the computer of the personality. It receives information from each of the five senses and processes that information in an organized and rational way. The early beginnings of Adult thinking start around the end of the second year of life as the infant's verbal abilities increase. The Adult ego state continues to develop through childhood, especially at school, until puberty when abstract and logical thinking become fully available (Piaget and Inhelder 1969). It collects, stores, and uses information in a factual kind of way without feeling, like a computer does, which separates it from the Child ego state, which has lots of feelings. It uses information to make assessments and calculate probabilities. It does not form opinions, which is the function of the Parent ego state, and Adult thinking is seen to occur in the left hemisphere of the brain.

This ego state is central for normal psychological functioning. The stronger it is the more likely the person will make accurate decisions. For instance, a person may feel worthless and of little status. This is a Child ego state feeling and not an Adult ego state assessment. Her Adult knows she is not worthless, that she is a valuable person who has every right to live a full life like everyone else. The stronger the Adult the less impact the Child ego state faulty beliefs will have on her behavior.

The Child ego state

The Child ego state is where the feelings, primal drives, and childlike aspects of us remain. In all of us there is an "inner child" that remains with us to our dying day. Sometimes it remains unchanged, with the feelings and thoughts one had in childhood staying with us and interfering with our everyday life in adulthood. If as a child life was scary and frightening, then in adulthood the person may develop anxiety conditions like phobias or repetitive nightmares. Feelings like anger, sadness, shame, hunger, thirst, sex, and joy are all part of the Child ego state. Whereas the Parent ego state is about copying, the Child ego state is about reacting.

CASE STUDY 3.2: CHILD EGO STATE

A 25-year-old female reports that she was raised in England and how she always hated boarding school. Much of her primary and secondary schooling was in boarding school. She also notes that her parents only lived a 15-minute drive from the school. She could have easily commuted to and from school each day but she was made a boarder and states that she hated it and always wanted to go home to her parents. It puzzled her why she had to be a boarder when other children who also lived near by did not. Every day she hated being at school. The food was horrible and she just wanted to be at home with her parents.

Her Child ego state inevitably reacted to being placed in boarding school and had to make some kind of sense of it. She concluded that there must be something wrong with her as her parents did not want her at home. The Child ego state reacted by reaching such a conclusion. She could not make an Adult ego state decision because as a young child the Adult ego state was not properly formed.

The Child ego state reacted in the way it did with feelings of anger, concluding she was not wanted by her parents. These remained with her until she entered counseling at age 25.

Ego states and the newborn child

When a child is born it only has the Child ego state part of the personality. The Adult and Parent ego states are not formed, so the newborn can only react to the world with this aspect of the personality. However, the Child ego state is actually subdivided into three separate ego states itself:

- the Child in the Child ego state (C1), also known as the Somatic Child

- the Adult in the Child ego state (A1), also known as the Little Professor

- the Parent in the Child ego state (P1), also known as the Electrode.

(Modified from Woollams and Brown 1978)

These are shown in Figure 3.3. This theory is essential to understanding how early childhood decisions occur.

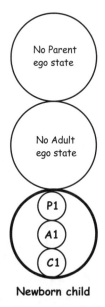

Newborn child

Figure 3.3 The three ego states within the Child ego state

THE C1 OR SOMATIC CHILD EGO STATE

The C1 or Somatic Child ego state is what the newborn brings into the world after all its experiences in the womb combined with its natural temperament. It contains all the feelings and urges along with the other needs for food, warmth, affection, security, and so forth. It is called the Somatic Child because it is focused on the body and bodily needs. The very young child has very little verbal capacity and thus the body does the talking for it. Pleasure and pain, bodily feelings of frustration, or feelings of warmth, colic, joy, and tiredness. Adults who are said to have pre-verbal issues had problems at this very early stage of life in their attachment with their main parenting figures. With a disrupted attachment the newborn will have bodily reactions and these remain in the body of the person, often for a lifetime.

For instance, if the infant feels hungry, cries, but no one comes, then it begins to cry less and remembers those experiences in its body. In adulthood this person can become a compulsive eater because of the unmet needs all those years ago. She has a constant feeling of hunger in her body, which is the Somatic Child ego state remembering that unmet need. When asked to describe it or talk about it the person will have difficulty because it is a bodily memory that is pre-verbal. The person will report that she cannot find the words to explain it but she can feel it in her body. These experiences of the Somatic Child can be recalled many years later, as they remain with us all our lives.

THE A1 OR LITTLE PROFESSOR EGO STATE

The A1 or the Adult in the Child ego state is sometimes known as the Little Professor ego state because it is the little thinker in the young child. Research tends to show that conscious thinking begins about the third month of life. At that point the child's thinking tends to be immature, magical, intuitive, creative, and curious. She displays an interest in herself and the world, and begins Little Professor thinking about what she sees, hears, and touches. Such young children can get quite engrossed in thinking and learning about toys and their bodies. When they develop the beginnings of speech they ask many, many, questions, which also shows their thinking ability.

However, the thinking is not like the grown up Adult ego state. This is pre-logical thinking that tends to occur on the right side of the brain and thus the youngster can reach some quite odd conclusions because she does not think in a logical systematic way. For instance, the A1 will demonstrate magical thinking, as is shown in Case study 3.2 above. The young girl concluded that there was something wrong with her and that was why her parents did not want her at home. Adults know this is not the case as there is nothing intrinsically wrong with a young child, but the Little Professor ego state does not have access to such logical and grown-up thinking.

Indeed, in psychoses like schizophrenia many of the thought disorders are precisely this. The Adult ego state is nonfunctioning, so the psychotic is left with only Little Professor thinking. Hence one gets symptoms like magical thinking, ideas of reference, loosening of association, tangentiality, and so forth. All these can occur when the Little Professor is processing information and the grown up Adult ego state is not available, as is the case with young children. The problem is that people make most of their major life decisions about the value of self and others when they have only Little Professor information processing and very little Adult ego state thinking. Hence they can make unfortunate decisions, as shown in Case study 3.2.

In subsequent counseling the woman in Case study 3.2 came to the realization that her mother was a narcissistic woman. The reason why she was sent to boarding school was because her mother wanted to have a life largely free of any child-rearing responsibilities. She could achieve this by sending her daughter to boarding school under the guise of doing it because she wanted her daughter to get a good education, thus maintaining respect amongst her peers. The grown up Adult ego state can understand that, whereas the Little Professor ego state is simply not capable of such sophisticated thinking, and thus she ended up making the decision that she was of little worth.

THE P1 OR ELECTRODE EGO STATE

The P1 or the Parent in the Child ego state is sometimes known as the Electrode. The two case studies presented above are just two examples of what happens many times in a child's life. Parents relate in consistent patterns to their children and thus the child will tend to make the same sort of decisions over and over again. When the Little Professor makes a decision it is stored away in the P1 or Electrode. As the same sort of decisions get made they are reinforced over and over again, until eventually the child will react automatically to events that happen in life. The child eventually does not need to make new decisions and will react automatically based on the decisions that are already in place in the Electrode ego state.

That is why it is called the Electrode, to indicate the automatic nature of the process. By the time the child is six years old it will simply respond automatically to new distressing events based on what is stored in the Electrode. For example, in Case study 3.2 the girl decided that she was placed in the boarding school because there was something wrong with her. She concluded that her parents put her there because of some failing in her and this decision was placed in the Electrode. When she grows into an adult woman she of course takes all these early decisions with her, often unconsciously. Most people are not even aware of the decisions they have in the Electrode.

At age 30, one day she is told at work that she is going to be shifted to a new department, which in essence is a demotion. The boss is doing this because of office politics and he has to put a new person into her current role so as to satisfy his superiors. He does not want to move her as she is a good worker. However, in her mind she has an automatic response from the decision in the Electrode. She automatically concludes she is being moved because of some failing in her, that there is something wrong with her, and she has not done the right things at work. This will be her automatic response and demonstrates the way the Electrode functions.

The functional ego states

The ego states described above show how the ego states are structured. This section will describe how the three ego states function. The ego states can be divided into six main functional ego states, as shown in Figure 3.4.

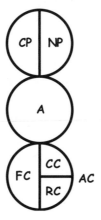

Figure 3.4 The functional ego states of the personality

THE PARENT EGO STATE

The Parent ego state can be divided into two parts:

1. *Critical Parent ego state (CP)*. Blames, attacks, criticizes, set limits and takes control. It tends to be judgmental and moralistic and uses words like must, should, ought to, and bad. It's like the critical father telling off the children for their bad behavior.

2. *Nurturing Parent ego state (NP)*. Helpful, caring, comforts, and rescues others. It tends to be giving, caring, comforting, accepting, and says words like I love you, nice, and cute. It's like the nurturing mother who is caring for a distressed child.

THE ADULT EGO STATE

Adult ego state (A). Listens, observes, is objective, organizes, and solves problems. It tends to be observant and evaluative, and says words like why, what, how, correct, and incorrect.

THE CHILD EGO STATE

The Child ego state is divided into two parts: the Free Child ego state and the Adapted Child ego state. The Adapted Child ego state can then be further subdivided into the Conforming Child ego state and the Rebellious Child ego state.

1. *Free Child ego state (FC)*. Feelings, has wants, spontaneous, intuitive, intimate. It tends to be curious, uninhibited, and says words like I'm angry, wow, fun, and ouch. It's like a young child running free on the beach or a child crying because her goldfish just died.

2. *Adapted Child ego state (AC)*. This part of us adapts to authority. It can do this in one of two ways, as shown by the Conforming and Rebellious ego states.

   (1) *Conforming Child ego state (CC)*. Pleases others, conforms, obeys. It tends to be compliant, do what it is told, is pleasing, innocent, and says words like please, thank you, yes, and may I. It's like the young child who is cleaning up her room or sitting quietly waiting for mummy to finish what she is doing.

(2) *Rebellious Child ego state (RC).* Oppositional, defiant, naughty, anti-authority. It tends to be demanding, pouting, sulky, and says words like no, get away, I won't do it, and try and make me. It's like the child sitting at the dinner table with her lips tightly closed and refusing to eat her food.

The RC is seen as an adaption to authority because it is adapting by doing the opposite. It still is not doing what it wants, like the FC does, but is just doing the opposite to what it is being told to do. For example, the RC will refuse to eat its dinner even if it is hungry, whereas the FC would eat the food.

Transactions

Whereas ego states provide a theory of personality, transactions provide a theory of human communication and relationships. A transaction consists of two communications, a stimulus and a response, as is shown in Figure 3.5.

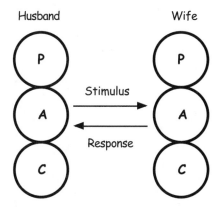

Figure 3.5 The two parts of a transaction

In this example we have two people, a husband and wife. The husband starts the first part of the transaction with the stimulus, "What is the time?" He is stating the question from his Adult ego state and is directing it at her Adult ego state. She responds with, "It is 9.30 am." She gives her response from her Adult to his Adult and the transaction is complete. Transactions can be sent from any ego state and be directed to any ego state, as shown in Figure 3.6.

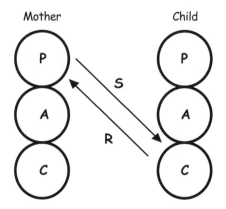

**Figure 3.6 A transaction between the
Parent and Child ego states**

The stimulus (S) is made by the mother from her Parent ego as she is trying to get the young child to eat dinner, "You are a naughty boy, open your mouth and eat your food." The response (R) from the child is from his RC, where he has his lips closed and grunts, "No!"

Figure 3.7 shows another type of transaction.

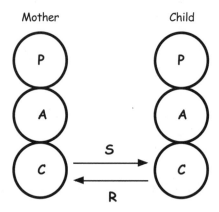

Figure 3.7 A transaction between the two Child ego states

In this case the mother may give the stimulus (S) from her Child ego state with, "Let's have a food fight!" The response (R) from the young child may be, "Yaaay! That sounds like fun."

As mentioned above, transactions can go from any ego state to any other ego state with a stimulus and a response in each instance.

Transactional analysis theory of dependence and addiction

In Chapter 1 different models of addiction were described, and it was shown that transactional analysis falls into the category of the psychodynamic view of addiction. This chapter will explain in much more detail how the transactional analysis model can explain the dynamics of addiction and drug dependence.

The transactional analysis theory of addiction comprises two parts, symbiosis and attachment. These have been presented elsewhere by White (1997a, 1998) but not discussed in terms of addiction.

Addiction and symbiosis

The symbiosis aspect of addiction can be represented by Figure 3.8.

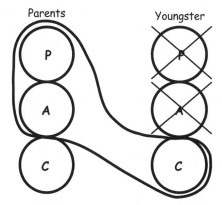

Figure 3.8 Symbiosis diagram of the addictive personality

Figure 3.8 shows the young child is born with only the Child ego state. The Parent and Adult ego states are yet to be formed and as such it has to develop a symbiosis to a fully grown person in order to survive physically and psychologically. In essence it borrows its mother's Parent and Adult ego states until it can grow its own. In normal human development this process gains completion in the late teens and early twenties. By that time the person has developed enough Parent and Adult ego to be able to survive physically and psychologically without the parents' help.

Sometimes this does not occur. The Parent and Adult ego states either do not form in any significant way or they are malformed.

If that is the case, then the person remains in a dependent state of mind. She does not psychologically grow up or develop a psychological independence which is provided by her own Adult and Parent ego states. For example, people need the Parent and Adult ego states for such tasks as self-soothing. When the Child ego state gets distressed it is the two other ego states that are used to soothe it. If they do not exist in a useable form the person either stays distressed or employs someone else to soothe her. The inability of the addict to self-soothe has been noted by many in the addictions literature: Kissen (2006), Krystal (1978), and O'Connor (1996).

Krystal (1978) supports what is being said here about the lack of the Parent ego state. He says that the substance-dependent patient has the self-caring functions of the maternal object representation inaccessible to her. Restated in transactional analysis terms, as shown in Figure 3.2, the Parent ego state of the substance-dependent person never introjected a soothing parental recording into her Parent ego state. As a consequence she has no soothing Parent ego state recording to use when her own Child ego state is distressed. She lacks a significant Nurturing Parent ego state that can be directed at her own Child ego state. Figure 3.9 shows what the substance-dependent person may lack—the ability to use NP on oneself.

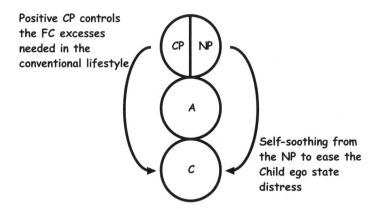

Figure 3.9 To self-soothe the person uses internal NP transactions. To control excessive Child wants and needs, the positive aspect of the CP is used internally in the personality. The CP sets boundaries and allows for self-control

Having malformed or nonexistent Parent and Adult ego states means the wants and excesses of the Child ego state are not controlled. This makes it very difficult for the person to live a conventional lifestyle, which is another feature of some dependent drug users, whose lives can be quite chaotic. To get a job or a mortgage, have a family, or save money for a car all require the Free Child ego state to be controlled by the logic of the Adult ego state and the moral values of the Parent ego state. The Free Child is a hedonistic part of the personality and if the individual finds drugs give her a desirable sense of euphoria, then she will want such drugs often. Most people control such hedonism with their Parent and Adult ego states and thus do not develop heavy drug use patterns or lifestyles with little responsibility.

Thus we have the personality structure of the addictive personality: an active Child ego state with malformed Parent and Adult ego states by which to control it and self-soothe. As a consequence the drug user will seek out another person or thing to take on the personality functions of her own Parent and Adult ego states and form a symbiosis with that. Drugs can do this well for some.

When one listens to dependent drug users talk about their drug one notes an uncanny similarity to a person talking about a husband or wife. The qualities of the relationship with the drug are similar to the qualities one finds in a relationship with a spouse or a parent, as described below. The drug users have formed a symbiosis with the drug in the same way a child forms a symbiosis with its mother.

When a child cries because it has gas, is hungry, or needs a change mother comes along, performs the appropriate task, the problem is solved and the child feels soothed. A 20-year-old heroin user may feel distressed, but is not capable of self-soothing, so she uses her drug. Almost instantly she feels better and soothed just like a child does when its mother does her job. The drug has taken on the Parent and Adult ego state tasks and forms that part of her personality. Thus we have the psychological basis of addictive drug taking. It should be noted that this connection between addictive relationships and an addiction to drugs has been discussed elsewhere by Moss (1982), White (1999), and Wilkinson and Saunders (1996).

Indeed, this was suggested a long time ago by Eric Berne (1957), the originator of transactional analysis. He states that the alcoholic does not have two-way relationships, instead she has relationships where she can lean on others and this is the same kind of relationship a person has with their mother. "He loved her because of what she did for him and not for herself...alcoholics are childlike in their emotional behavior... In fact, it is no joke to say that the alcoholic is a person who has never been weaned from the bottle" (p.215).

It has been shown here that the dependent individual can form a symbiosis with another person or a drug, but there are other possibilities, such as with an organization or even a belief system. I saw many examples of this when I worked in a prison system. No one likes being in prison but some people are comfortable there. There are a significant group of inmates who are simply incapable of existing on the outside in any reasonable kind of way for any significant length of time. When they are released their lack of Adult or Parent ego state control over the Child ego state results in them eventually running amok, breaking the law, and getting caught. One sees reports of men who go on crime sprees, such as doing a series of armed robberies, often whilst intoxicated. You cannot do that for any length of time and not get caught, and eventually most do. They usually get identified quickly by security cameras, the police know who they are, and usually find them quite quickly amongst their known associates. This type of crime can be reflective of a person who has a lack of Parent and Adult ego states. They make little if any attempt to seriously cover their tracks or identity, knowing they are eventually going to get caught and imprisoned. Eventually they end up in prison, where the prison performs those personality functions for them. It places them on a strict routine, feeds them, houses them, washes them, employs them, and so forth. The inmate forms a symbiosis with the prison. It becomes his Parent and Adult ego states.

CASE STUDY 3.3: SYMBIOSIS

A 27-year-old man, spending his ninth year in prison, grew up in a large city as an only child. His mother left when he was just a baby and he never met her. His father was a hard-working man who also drank a lot. He provided all the necessary things for him like food and clothing but had little interest in having a relationship with him. He placed no controls on his son. This man spent his childhood and adolescence doing what he wanted. At age ten he would leave the home, often for days at a time, and his father never questioned him on this.

This man in essence grew up without a Parent ego state developing as he never had any parent-type figures around him to model and copy from. At age 19 he was imprisoned for seven years on drug offences. He does "good" time and causes very few problems for the prison system. When the time for his release was getting closer he murdered another inmate and was sentenced to another 18 years.

This man became well known to me and he was always polite and friendly. He provides a good example of developing a symbiosis with the prison system and he indeed acknowledged this. He reported liking the routine and that he did not have any goals or ideas about what he wanted with life. The prison provided his Parent and Adult ego states, which made him feel more secure and reluctant to give up. However, this needs to be distinguished from institutionalization. Any person living in a prison for months or years is going to become institutionalized to some degree, as the institution has such a large impact on their day to day lives. However, only a small number will take the institution on as a means to solve their own personality maladaptions.

In summary, the first part of the transactional analysis theory of drug addiction involves the drug performing various functions of the personality of the individual. Once this occurs it solves some very real and difficult problems for the individual such as the inability to self-soothe. Addiction to drugs like methadone and cannabis can also allow people to live less chaotic and more conventional lifestyles. Thus the individual will be reluctant to give those up and hence can be seen to be addicted to the drug. This theory of drug addiction focuses on the relationship the user has with the drug rather than it being a social learning process or a disease.

Addiction and attachment

The second aspect of addiction in this theory is the idea of attachment. Much has been written on this since John Bowlby (1971) presented the idea with his ground-breaking work on the topic in the 1950s. In that book Bowlby attempted to distinguish between dependency and attachment, because many at that time viewed them as closely related.

He said that a child is dependent on adults for food and shelter. This was distinct from attachment, which he behaviorally defined as the "desire to maintain proximity." A child who is attached to its mother has a very strong desire to remain close to her geographically. One knows when a child has formed an attachment to its mother because it will exhibit proximity-seeking behavior. It will spend time and effort to remain in close geographical proximity to its mother. Indeed, if necessary, it will expend vast amounts of time and effort to do so, even almost to the point of death. (Never underestimate the power of human attachment and this desire to maintain proximity, it is an awesome force in human behavior.) Bowlby saw attachment purely in these behavioral terms.

Since then others have added to the theory, as a purely behavioral definition of attachment is seen as limited. As a case in point, consider someone you have a strong attachment to. Is there more to your relationship than simply a desire to maintain proximity with the other? I think it is safe to say that most would answer "Yes." Subsequent writers such as Margaret Mahler (1965) and Mahler, Pine, and Bergman (1975) say that attachment also involves a sense of identity. The other becomes part of how one views oneself. They become part of the identity. How this can happen is explained in Figure 3.2 above. A husband and wife who live together over time will introject the other into their own Parent ego state. They introject the personality of the other into oneself such that it becomes part of their own identity. This gives a much fuller theory of attachment, including the desire to maintain proximity plus a merging of identities. The person you have a strong attachment to has been introjected into your Parent ego state such that their personality is now part of yours. Thus it seems safe to say that any attachment also involves some degree of dependency. One is dependent on the other to maintain proximity and because they represent part of one's very own identity.

Most people as they grow, go through the normal attachment and separation process with their primary parenting figure. This can be shown in Figure 3.10.

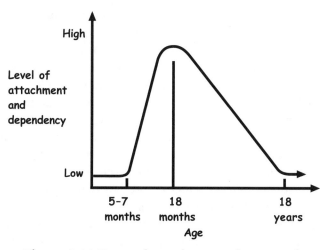

Figure 3.10 Dependency hump—the normal attachment and separation process

At about five to seven months of age the child begins to establish its first discernible attachments. Hence its level of attachment to its mother rises dramatically and reaches a peak at about 18–24 months of age (White 1997a). At this point the child is very dependent on mother to maintain proximity and the child's own sense of identity is intimately intertwined with its mother's personality. The loss of its mother at this point can have a very significant impact on a child's psychological development. After that age it begins the separation process and spends the next 16 years trying to break that attachment down. If successfully achieved, at about 18 years of age it achieves what Mahler *et al.* (1975) called the psychological birth. It becomes a psychologically discrete person on its own. In essence, the child combines its sense of self with its mother's personality for the first 18 years of life until it can fully develop its own.

Some, however, do not successfully traverse the dependency hump and hence end up with attachment disorders of various kinds in adulthood. These have been given various names over the years, such as reactive attachment disorder, disorganized attachment, insecure attachment, ambivalent attachment, and so forth. Some children never make it up the hump in the first place. In the extreme this is found in the autistic child, who for whatever reason never develops any significant attachments. Most do in varying degrees and as a result could be seen to progress up the graph.

To do so successfully there must be an affectionate, emotionally available adult in the child's life who is present at least relatively consistently. Sometimes this does not happen. The mother may have her own drug problems, have a mental illness such as postnatal depression, be quite narcissistic, or simply be incapable of making emotional contact with the child. When the primary parenting figure is not emotionally available to the child we get the "hurried child syndrome." This child may be given all the practicalities, such as food and shelter, but is left to emotionally fend for itself and as a result the attachment with its mother is disrupted. The child has to hurry and grow up before it is emotionally and psychologically ready.

On the other hand the child may make it to the top but for some reason it is not allowed to psychologically separate and thus never makes it successfully down the other side. Its mother may have smothered the child or for some reason does not allow the child to psychologically develop and break away from her. An example of this is shown in Case study 3.4.

CASE STUDY 3.4: *PROBLEM ATTACHMENT*

A 38-year-old woman presents to counseling with panic attacks and an addiction to prescription Valium. She finds her life is quite debilitating and seems to be in a state of constant worry. In discussion over time she talks about her only child, a ten-year-old boy. It becomes apparent quite quickly there are problems with him and in her relationship with him, although she never presents these as problems.

Since he started school he has often refused to go and he is in real terms home schooled by his mother. She often puts him to bed for an afternoon sleep, prevents him from riding his bike away from home because its too dangerous, and discourages him from making friends because the other boys are too rough and bully him. Most nights he sleeps in mother's bed with her. After further discussion it is disclosed that she had two miscarriages prior to his birth and one other since he was born. The parents are no longer trying for children. The boy now displays strong signs of separation anxiety disorder and often refuses to leave his mother's close proximity. This boy is not successfully separating from his mother and thus is stuck at the top of the dependency graph. If this should continue, then one of the keys to later drug addiction is in place.

In examples such as this the person never successfully traverses the hump, and is left with attachment and dependency problems, thus forming the psychological basis for other dependencies developing later in life, possibly adulthood drug and alcohol dependencies. The role of attachment disorders and subsequent drug use problems have been mentioned by others (Brennan and Shaver 1995; Cooper, Shaver and Collins 1998; Reinhart and Edwards 2009). Indeed a study by De Rick, Vanheule, and Vanhaeghe (2009) found that 86 percent of alcoholic inpatients they researched had disrupted attachment styles in their relationships in varying degrees.

When working as a drug counselor one quickly finds addicted drug users display very strong proximity-seeking behavior to the drug. In addition many suffer from the self-perception of being a "junkie." Their relationship with the drug allows them to take on the identity of being a junkie. If they stop using, of course, that aspect of their identity changes into something else. Such people live with an excessive need for something to attach to. Sometimes it lurks in the background and at other times in their day to day life it will be in their consciousness, but it will persist in their psyche day in and day out. The Child ego state has that drive in them as the boy in Case study 3.4 will when he grows into a man. His Child ego state will have a persistent drive to finally resolve the dependency issues by traversing the dependency graph. It will remain with him at varying levels of consciousness until he does successfully complete the process. As Moss (1982) states, addiction in human relationships precedes addictions to drugs.

It should also be noted that the original dependency in the attachment with the mother may not change to a later addiction to drugs but can be an addiction to other things such as gambling or sex. Indeed it may even stay as an addiction to relationships in adulthood. This is highlighted in the *Diagnostic and Statistical Manual of Mental Disorders* (DSM-IV-TR) (American Psychiatric Association 2000), which talks about the dependent personality disorder.

Quotes taken from the diagnostic features of the dependent personality disorder include "clinging behavior and fears of separation…a self perception of being unable to function adequately without the help of others…unable to function alone…difficulty initiating projects or doing things independently…worry about being abandoned" (pp.721–722). One finds many of these features in drug users, such as being unable to cope without the drug, worrying about losing access to the drug and so forth. In the dependent personality disorder the person is addicted to another person rather than a drug as the same psychological processes are at work. As a consequence the dependent personality disorder in the DSM-IV-TR should not be seen as a personality disorder but instead as an addiction.

This theory of addiction describes how all children are born psychologically dependent in their primary attachment with their mother. Most grow out of this as part of normal child development over the formative years. Some do not and thus one ends up with people who are psychologically susceptible to addictions to drugs and alcohol. In reality this would seem to be one factor along with others, such as the disease view and the social learning view of addiction. If the person has a particular combination of these factors, then a serious drug addiction is possible in her lifetime. If not, she may develop other addictions such as gambling or sex addictions. If the person does not resolve her symbiosis and attachment to her mother but does not have a the right biochemical or genetic basis for alcoholism, then she may become a functional alcoholic, a person who can drink habitually and heavily most nights but still maintain a functional lifestyle and thus avoid the characteristics of what is usually seen as an alcoholic person. The same may apply in the other direction for the person who has the genetic propensity to addiction but has resolved her original symbiotic addiction to her mother and thus never develops a fully fledged drug or alcohol addiction.

Conclusion

This chapter gave a brief introduction to the theory of ego states and transactions. For the purposes of the book this is sufficient theory in order to explain the concepts necessary for working with drug and alcohol users. Also presented was the transactional analysis theory of addictions. It provides a different perspective to other theories such as the social learning theory or the psychoanalytic theory, highlighting the role of relationship and identity in the addiction process. Addiction to drugs is about an addictive relationship learnt in the childhood years. It is a relational process to the drug rather than a learning process such as in social learning theory. This of course has significant implications for treatment, as will become apparent in later chapters. Of course, in practice it seems unwise to simply stay with one view of addiction. It would be more appropriate to use a variety of approaches, especially the psychodynamic, social learning, and psychiatric, when dealing with different clients who each have different clinical circumstances.

Chapter 4

Why People Use Drugs and their Treatment

Introduction

People use drugs for a whole variety of different reasons. There have been many explanations for this over the years and a variety of differing "classification" systems have been presented. Presented here is a transactional analysis point of view and one which lends itself readily to the practicalities of drug and alcohol counseling. Initially it looks at alcohol use, as that is the most widely used and abused drug in most countries, then gives a description of illicit drug use and the different motives involved. Treatment plans for the various types of drug use are also described.

The effects of alcohol on personality

We have all seen how alcohol affects people, indeed most of us have experienced it first hand ourselves. The relaxation effects and sense of well being, allowing us to socialize more easily and talk more. The reduction of inhibitions makes for more enjoyment, but we may regret what we did or said the next day due to sexual behavior or aggression. With higher consumption comes slurring of speech, staggering, and possibly even vomiting, and then, of course, there is the hangover the next day. We have all at least seen this in others and it is not uncommon in most societies. Alcohol is the most widely used drug of all, and there follows an explanation of how to understand its effects in a more systematic way. Figure 4.1 shows the progressive effect that alcohol has on the personality. The different effects explain the differing motives people have for using alcohol.

As people consume alcohol, the ego states tend to disappear or become decommissioned. As one starts drinking, first the Parent ego state is decommissioned, as shown in Figure 4.1a. Even after just a few drinks the Parent ego state becomes less influential in the personality. Most importantly the Critical Parent ego state becomes silent. For many people this makes alcohol most attractive.

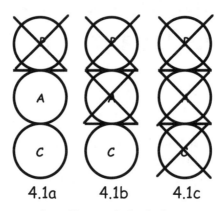

4.1a   4.1b   4.1c

Figure 4.1 The effects of alcohol on personality

Most people when they go to a social event like a party may think: "Who will be there?", "Do I look OK?", "What will I talk about?", "Will I know anyone?", and so on. Meeting and being with people who are either unknown or superficially known to us in a social setting is not an easy exercise. Most humans struggle with it to some degree and it can bring out some of our insecurities. Most of these insecurities are generated from the Critical Parent ego state. Inside we are telling ourselves "I look fat," "My clothes are not right," "I can't carry on a reasonable conversation," "I'm not funny enough or smart enough," "Everybody is looking at me and judging me," and so on. Most of us have these insecurities to some degree but for a smaller group they have a very pronounced. Some have a very active and savage internal critic, which is often found in the depressed person. How this works in the personality is shown in Figure 4.2.

As Figure 4.2 shows, the internal Critical Parent ego state berates and criticizes the Child ego state. All of us do this to varying degrees, but for some, as stated above, these internal transactions can be relentless and particularly savage. With the consumption of even a small amount of alcohol those internal transactions are turned off or significantly reduced. This makes alcohol particularly appealing to those who have an active internal Critical Parent. The alcohol is quick acting, cheap, and effective in this way, and this is one of the reasons why it is so popular.

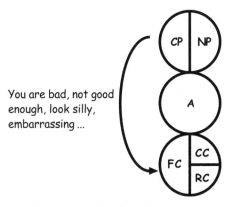

You are bad, not good enough, look silly, embarrassing ...

Figure 4.2 The internal Critical Parent transaction

The resultant effect when the Critical Parent is turned off is that the Free Child can come out to play, which is the other attractive reason for drinking alcohol. Alcohol is a disinhibitor and it is the Parent ego state that inhibits the Child ego state. With the Parent ego state reduced the person becomes less inhibited and the Free Child aspect of the personality becomes more influential. This explains why the hostess of a cocktail party makes sure there is plenty to drink early on in the night. She is worried that her party will not be a success and she knows that alcohol will allow the Free Child of her guests to come out and play. If that happens then the guests will "lighten up," the party will be an enjoyable evening for most, and it will be deemed a success.

However, there are other effects when alcohol decommissions the Parent ego state. The Parent ego state controls the urges of the Child ego state and that includes the sexual and aggressive urges. If one's morals and values are minimized, as they are with alcohol, a person can behave in ways which they would normally not. That can involve sexual behavior, which they rue the next day when the Parent ego state is re-energized and chastizes the Child ego state for behaving outside its usual moral code. Indeed this internal Critical Parent chastizement is a prominent part of many a hangover, in addition to the physical sense of unwellness.

The same applies for aggressive behavior. The young adult male has parental values so that he would not normally physically punch another person. When those are taken away, he is disinhibited to act on the Child ego state urge to physically hit out when he is angry, just like a six-year-old child does. This is one reason why alcohol plays a prominent part in many domestic violence situations. However, if the person has only consumed a small amount of alcohol, then the Adult ego state is still operational, as shown in Figure 4.1a. This means he is still capable of making good Adult decisions. For example, the young adult male may have his Parent ego state values minimized, but his Adult ego state can decide not to punch out because he knows he may get punched back or may even be charged with assault. Thus the Free Child aggressive urge is halted because of an Adult decision rather than the Parent ego state value system.

If he consumes more alcohol, then the Adult ego state is also decommissioned as shown in Figure 4.1b. He is left with only his Child ego state functioning. His moral code is gone, his ability to make wise decisions is also gone, and the Free Child is allowed to roam as it wishes. While that can feel very nice to some, especially the highly inhibited person and the depressed person, it is a potentially volatile situation, especially when it comes to sexual and aggressive behaviors. The person has few controls over what they do or say. Indeed, if you wish to find out what a friend really thinks of you, invite them over, get them drunk, and then ask. With the Adult and Parent ego states gone the usual censorship of what they would say is also gone and they will speak more truly of their feelings from the Free Child. This is why some people are happy drunks, sad drunks, or angry drunks. The true feelings of the Free Child are allowed to surface when the censorship is taken away.

If the person continues to drink, eventually the Child ego state is decommissioned and he passes out or in some way becomes incapacitated. At that point the person has no conscious functioning in his personality, as shown in Figure 4.1c. He is completely vulnerable to assault or theft of some kind. On the other hand, if he has terrible memories from combat in a war zone or memories of very bad abuse in childhood, then the state shown in Figure 4.1c allows for a temporary respite from those memories and feelings. Many of those who have post-traumatic stress disorder (PTSD) can suffer chronic insomnia, or even when they do sleep are plagued by recurrent and very distressing nightmares. If all the ego states are decommissioned by alcohol then at least one can sleep and sleep without the nightmares.

Reasons for using drugs

Some of the effects and reasons why people use alcohol were examined above. This section will put the main reasons why people use alcohol and other illicit drugs into an overall context. It begins with the more benign forms of drug use, leading up to the more problematic types of use.

Experimental drug use

In this instance people take the drug as an experiment to see what it is like. Obviously this is the first time(s) the person uses the drug, making it a short type of drug use. People will either stop using or move on to another type of drug use. As a result this type of drug use often occurs in the teens or early twenties. However, it can occur at other times, as with a mid-life crisis when a 40-year-old man experiments with marijuana for the first time. It is usually associated with a new developmental stage in a person's life. When a person moves to a new stage of development he often experiments with a variety of new things, including drug use.

If a person smokes marijuana one to ten times, that can be considered experimental use. If the person keeps using, then the type of use changes. Some people stop after experimenting just a few times. With marijuana it is not uncommon to hear people say they tried it and it just made them paranoid so they stopped. Others say it just made them feel sick; for some reason the drug does not agree with the person's body chemistry and the experience is unpleasant, as mentioned in Chapter 2 when discussing the drug of choice.

The goal of experimental use is precisely that, to experiment and find out what this thing called cannabis or cocaine feels like. Once they have used a few times they have experimented and thus the reason disappears. As the drug use is new the source of supply can be quite unreliable. It may have come from a friend of a friend of a friend, so experimental drug use can be quite erratic as the supply is erratic and the quality is often quite poor as they are at the bottom of the food chain at that point. Peers and peer groups often play a significant role in this type of drug use. Teenagers watch some of their peers smoke marijuana and then wonder what it would be like for them.

COUNSELING THE EXPERIMENTAL USER

The main ego states that are active in this type of drug use are the Free Child, Rebellious Child, and possibly the Adult ego state. It is these aspects of the personality that result in such experimentation. Experimental users rarely seek counseling for their drug use because they do not view it as a problem. They may attend drug counseling as coerced clients because they have been caught out and their parents make them attend. Alternatively such drug use can be mentioned as a kind of side issue by a person who is already in counseling for other reasons. A young adult female may come to counseling for insomnia, depression, or perhaps an eating disorder and will mention in one session that she tried marijuana last week or is thinking of trying it because her friends are.

The counselor's role is to provide basic information about drugs and drug use, as described in Chapter 2, basically to provide an education program to the client, which may include providing reading matter. A counselor would also engage in harm minimization counseling, which will be discussed in detail in Chapter 5. It is imperative that the counselor does not lie to the client about the effects and dangers of drugs, as was discussed in Chapter 2. The information needs to be the truth and the whole truth, but of course presented in a way suitable for the age of the client.

Counseling should also look at the role of the peer group with experimental drug users, especially if they are in their teens or early twenties. Is the client a leader or a follower in relation to the peers? Sometimes there can be considerable peer pressure to use drugs, which they are ambivalent about, and counseling obviously would focus on those issues as well. With the younger age group the developmental task at hand is leaving home and separating from the parents. Is the experimental drug use reflecting some of that developmental task? Is the drug being taken so that the teenager feels separate and different to his parents? Drug counseling in this instance needs to look at the possibility of these dynamics playing a part as well.

Rebellious drug use

As soon as something is banned there will be a group of people who want to try it. Everyone has a Rebellious Child ego state that will react rebelliously when told it cannot do something. Of course, some people have a small RC and others have a big RC. In particular people in the teenage years tend to have a large RC ego state and thus the rebellious type of drug use often occurs in the teenage stage of development.

This type of drug use can be much longer than experimental use, lasting a number of years as the person goes through a rebellious phase. Indeed some people maintain an active rebellious attitude their entire lives. However, there is a group who tend to grow out of it in their late teens or early twenties. Typically there may be marijuana or tobacco use for five or six years and then the person loses interest in it. People will tend to grow out of this type of drug use as they pass through their rebellious developmental phase. However, others have the Rebellious Child active in their personality for many years and these people are seen to take drugs from a rebellious position. An example is shown in Case study 4.1.

CASE STUDY 4.1: REBELLIOUS CHILD

The following dialogue comes from an interview I had with a 52-year-old woman with a long history of chronic tobacco addiction. In the parentheses is my thinking at the time.

Therapist: I am interested in why you smoke, what is it that you get out of smoking, such that you do not stop?

(I am looking for the Child ego state reason for her smoking)

Client: Don't tell me not to smoke. I will smoke if I want to. Who do you think you are to tell me not to smoke. I enjoy smoking. Fuck off and leave me alone.

(I get an immediate Rebellious Child ego state response)

After a bit of time she calms down and we continue.

T: OK. What are the advantages of it?

C: Habit, too hard to stop, I like smoking.

T: What do you like about it?

C: I like the...don't know. Maybe it's just habit. It's stop time. I don't know, it just feels nice, stop time is time out. It's...like between classes at school. I go for a wander, have a smoke, and get time out. It's alone for that as well. I must admit I've never really thought about what I like about it.

(I get a bit of the Child ego state reasons for smoking)

T: What do you feel about smoking?

C: I feel good about smoking. Course there's always now, the bit that says I shouldn't smoke. Particularly with all the adverts about quitting, etc. There's a lot more of that now than in the past. In the past there was less of the "I should" stop.

(she now identifies the strong presence of her Critical Parent ego state in the reasons why she is smoking)

T: Is there are part of you that wants to stop.

(I am being persistent in trying to get to the Child ego state reasons for smoking but with not much luck)

C: I don't know if there is a part that actually wants to stop. I think it's more of a should. Before all the whooo ha about smoking, there was never any feeling of wanting to quit.

(again she identifies the strong presence of the Critical Parent ego state)

T: So there really is very little FC investment in stopping?

C: Yah, I think so.

T: Which would explain why you have not stopped?

C: Yah, and as I say, very high RC investment. Particularly now with all the shit about stopping, how bad it is for you, and the social outcast stuff, so for me, all the adverts, etc. are just making it worse.

In this case it was not so much about the good part or the advantages of smoking, although there was a bit when she reported that smoking allowed her to get stop time and alone time in between teaching her classes at school. This is what one usually gets when asking such questions, and what I persisted in trying to ascertain, only to eventually give up. With this type of drug user it is more about defiance and rebellion as the motivation to smoke. The main advantage she got from smoking was to defy authority, which includes her own internal Critical Parent ego state.

While this is more common in the young, as this case study shows, any adult person who has a strong rebellious side to his personality has the potential to take drugs habitually from a rebellious position. In this type of user there is a set of transactions that becomes ingrained in the communication patterns. There is an ingrained pattern of Critical Parent to Rebellious Child transactions which can occur in two ways, as shown in Figure 4.3.

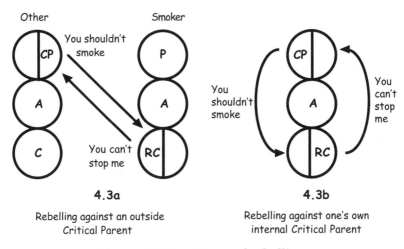

4.3a

Rebelling against an outside
Critical Parent

4.3b

Rebelling against one's own
internal Critical Parent

Figure 4.3 Two types of rebellious transactions about smoking cigarettes

In Figure 4.3a the drug user has an external person (or organization) which they perceive as a Critical Parent telling them they should stop smoking. Often this will be someone like a mother or father, spouse, parole officer, or even a counselor who is saying precisely that. If this has been going on for some time, then the transaction becomes ingrained in the communication pattern between the two parties. This is a negative thing to happen if one is working with a rebellious type of drug user as it simply perpetuates the drug use. To make matters more difficult the external person does not even have to be coming from her Critical Parent ego state, it all depends on how the drug user perceives it, as shown in Case study 4.1. My initial statement as the therapist was an Adult to Adult ego state transaction, but her rebellious response indicates that she perceived it as a Critical Parent transaction, which in her mind automatically sets up the habitual transactions that she is used to. She also states that she perceives government health warnings against smoking on television to be Critical Parent, which, as she states, just encourages the smoking, indeed she reports that it makes it worse.

Figure 4.3b shows how over time the external Critical Parent views of smoking get introjected into the user's own Parent ego state.

When this happens she does not even need an external Critical Parent and will set up her own ingrained internal set of transactions between the Critical Parent and Rebellious Child ego states. Each time this transaction occurs the rebellious drug user gets further reinforcement to use. This may happen many, many times each day as she lights up each new cigarette, making the reinforcement persistent and powerful.

COUNSELING THE REBELLIOUS USER

More will be said on this topic later, when counseling the teenage drug user is discussed in Chapter 10, as many of the rebellious drug users are of that age. However, as Case study 4.1 shows, there certainly are older drug users who use from a rebellious position. This identifies the first thing one must do in counseling here: assess if the person is using drugs from a rebellious position, particularly with the younger drug user. This is not difficult to do and Case study 4.1 shows the basic process. Ask some Adult ego state questions such as: "Why do you use," "What do you use," "Tell me about your drug use," "What do you think about using drugs," etc.? If you get a rebellious response that is a sign the user takes drugs from a rebellious position, at least in part. Or just make a general assessment about how rebellious this person is in her everyday life.

A main counseling goal is to avoid getting into the transactional pattern described in Figure 4.3a, and that can be a difficult thing to achieve at times. First and foremost the counselor must be sure they are not in fact delivering a Critical Parent transaction to the client. They may think they are being Adult to Adult in their transactions but underneath there may be a critical view of the drug-using client which is being unconsciously delivered though subtle body language and the tone of voice. Assuming this is not the case, then the counselor can still be perceived as critical when they are not, which makes it difficult to stay out of the pattern shown in Figure 4.3a.

This type of drug user does not tend to voluntarily seek drug counseling. Most often they are either sent for counseling by someone else or they are in counseling for some other reason and the drug use gets mentioned in passing. However, a counselor counseling such a person needs to avoid becoming involved in the Critical Parent to Rebellious Child transactions. One needs to duck and weave through the incoming Rebellious Child prompts—at times the user may mention a few dangerous drug taking practices to try and get you to respond in a critical way. The counselor can be put in some quite difficult circumstances at times if the client is persistent at getting a Critical Parent ego state response.

The counselor can bring this to the awareness of the client, as with the transactions shown in Figure 4.3. In addition these transactions do not involve the Free Child ego state. The client is not doing what *they want to do*, but doing what *you do not want them to do*. They are trying to prove something to the other rather than doing what they want. The rebellious user may not even want to use but will continue to do so as defiance is of such importance to them. Again, more will be said about this when I discuss working with the teenage drug user.

Recreational drug use

This is by far the largest group of drug and alcohol users, and involves using drugs for recreational leisure activities or social purposes such as enhancing social interaction. This is more typical of adult drug taking over a long period of time, such as at the "cocktail party" or the "after work drink." It is primarily a function of the Free Child ego state. Most never come to the attention of health workers or the law.

This type of drug use is intermittent, where there is no major negative impact on the person and his family such as a health or financial problems. In this case the person gets the pleasurable effects and disinhibiting effects of the drug, used in a socializing way. Unlike the "drug addict" type of user, the recreational drug user does not feel he has to control his drug use. Instead he does not want to use the drug more frequently as he has a life outside drugs, such as family, work, hobbies, and so forth. There is no battle to control the drug use like the dependent user has, because the recreational user has a life beyond drugs.

This pattern of use can range from once or twice a week to once every a few months. Most drinkers are of this kind, where they will have a few drinks when they go out. There is never a period of escalation as occurs with the dependent user. *The Australian* (1997) reports there are between 50,000 and 150,000 recreational heroin users in Australia. These people never seek treatment and are able to maintain normal functioning lives. There may be times when they get a mild habit, but they are able stop using and get their lives back on a relatively drug-free track without too much trouble. This type of drug use can go on for many, many years. Many people can drink socially from age 16 to 80 without any serious harm to themselves or their lifestyle. The same can happen with many illicit drugs.

As heroin has such a reputation as an addictive drug that ruins lives, some find it odd to talk about recreational heroin use. However, there is clear evidence that such a group of people do exist. They can use heroin over a number of, if not many, years and never suffer the escalation of drug use that spirals them into heroin addiction (Best, Day *et al.* 2008). Sherwan and Dalgarno (2005) followed a group of 94 people who on average had been using heroin for seven years. Over that period of time their use never increased to levels where it was a harmful factor in their life. Thus any drug can be used recreationally, and this is further evidence that drugs do not grab people and drag them into addiction, as is often portrayed in movies. As highlighted in Chapter 3, on the theory of addiction, those who do develop drug addictions have a pre-existing personality structure that makes them susceptible to addiction.

COUNSELING THE RECREATIONAL USER

Recreational users do not usually seek treatment for their drug use, but should it arise in counseling, one again provides information on drugs, harm minimization, and so forth. The counselor may also engage in some discussion with the person as to when the drug use may become a problem. On some occasions, slowly over time the drug use may reach a point where it stops being recreational and becomes problem drug use. This can be discussed with the client, so that he gets an understanding of what indicators for him would show this change has taken place. One way of describing this is with the four Ls:

- Liver—health problems caused by the drug use

- Lover—relationship problems caused by the drug use

- Livelihood—financial problems caused by the drug use

- Legal—legal problems caused by the drug use.

Working with the client to define with more clarity what he sees as significant health, relationship, financial, and/or legal problems that are the result of his drug use has been put forward by Lauren Fricker, psychologist colleague (pers. comm. 2011). He can get more of a sense of that line between recreational and problem drug use. For example, if a man's wife has told him she will leave him unless he stops marijuana smoking, that does indicate a significant relationship problem generated by his drug use. If she only complains spasmodically and at times joins him in his smoking, then that is much less of a relationship problem. If she stops going out with him socially because his drinking embarrasses her that is also a problem for the relationship. Such discussions allow the client to define that line of dysfunctional drug use in terms of the effects it has on his relationships.

Alternatively one could counsel the drug user on what he sees as a reasonable amount to spend on drugs. Is it 1 percent of his income, 10 percent, or 30 percent? If he has been caught three times for drunk driving does that indicate dysfunctional alcohol use? If he is developing early warning signs of diabetes does that indicate problem alcohol use? It is these sorts of situations that the counselor can put to the recreational drug user, so that he can gain a more clear understanding of what recreational and problem drug use are for him. This type of drug use also raises the notion of the "functional drug user" or what is sometimes called the "functional alcoholic."

CASE STUDY 4.2: FUNCTIONAL ALCOHOLIC

A 30-year-old male rents a house with friends and is currently not in a relationship. He has relationships spasmodically but at this time he is not really interested in forming such a union. He drinks about a two-litre cask of red wine each night, seven days a week, and has done so for the past five years. He wakes up each day feeling sick, with a hangover which lasts until about lunchtime or early afternoon. He has missed work due to a particularly bad hangover only once or twice a year in the past few years. He has no known health concerns at this time and has never been in trouble with the law. He is in a highly paid job working as a geologist with a mining company and has no financial hardship.

The scenario presented in this case study is not all that uncommon. He consumes what would generally be considered a large amount of alcohol each day. On this basis alone some would call him an alcoholic. However, the effects of the alcohol on his day to day life are minimal. He can function quite effectively day to day while consuming the alcohol that he does. He would be seen by many as a functional alcoholic. Does he have a drinking problem? He has never sought to reduce his drinking since being in counseling, which he has attended on and off for the past three years.

CASE STUDY 4.3: *FUNCTIONAL DRUG ADDICT*

A 50-year-old male who is married with two grown children is a business man who has succeeded very well financially and continues to do so in the retail industry. He uses cocaine an average of three nights a week and has done so for many years. Most often it is done with his fellow business associates at evening meetings and dinners. His wife does not like it and complains about it from time to time. She has threatened to divorce him on a few occasions but has never followed up such threats in any serious way. He has never been in trouble with the law.

This man could be categorized as a functional drug addict. As with Case study 4.2, the volume of drugs consumed would be considered by some to clearly show this person has a drug problem. In any city one would be surprised at the number of high flyers in business, the professions, and government who use similar expensive party drugs in the same way as described in Case study 4.3. They would argue that it is recreational drug use, and do not view it as a problem because they have functioned that way for many years without any significant ill effects on their everyday life. Indeed, in financial and career terms, they have been highly successful.

These case studies illustrate that the line between recreational drug use and dysfunctional drug use is, at times, not a clear one. The counseling process with the recreational drug user is to present to the client the idea of the four Ls or the different ways drugs can impact one's life. Then facilitate discussion with the drug user to allow them to define what is functional and dysfunctional drug use for them. I recall working with a client who, in essence, used his drug use as a way to end his marriage. He wanted out of the marriage and eventually got his wife to leave by not adhering to her requests to reduce his drinking. Is that dysfunctional drug use? In his mind it was not at all.

Situational drug use

An example of this type of drug use is called "Dutch courage." The young man who is about to ask the father of his girlfriend if he can marry her will have a shot of whiskey to build up his courage to do so. The alcohol is used in a specific situation for a specific reason. If one has a bad day at work, when they get home they have a couple of beers to settle down. Again the alcohol is being used for a specific purpose. Truck drivers may use amphetamines to stay awake, as may the student who is studying for exams. A person may have a strong coffee in the morning to get him going or an artist use LSD for creativity. Drugs are used to beat boredom in prison or tranquilizers used to help with stage performances and auditions.

COUNSELING THE SITUATIONAL DRUG USER

As with the three previous types of drug users—experimental, rebellious, and recreational—the situational drug user rarely presents voluntarily for drug counseling. Like the others they do not see themselves as having a drug-use problem. As a consequence the person is either sent for counseling by some other person or organization, or the drug use arises as a side issue for someone who is already receiving counseling. The counselor would examine with the user other ways of dealing with stressful or difficult situations without having to use drugs. Once informed the client is then in a position to make his decision on whether to use the drug or some other kind of stress reduction method in the future. Finally, as with the other cases, one would also be providing information on drugs, their effects, harm minimization, and the line between functional and dysfunctional drug use.

It is the final two types of drug use discussed below that one most commonly finds in drug counseling and where most of the counseling resources are employed.

Symptomatic drug use

This is sometimes referred to as "self-medicating." People use the drug to avoid unpleasant experiences or memories or to avoid dealing with here and now challenges and responsibilities. The drug is used to numb the person or allows him to delay thinking about something and thus the symptom "goes away." While the first four groups are quite large in number, this type and the next are quite small in number. Almost any type of drug can be used for self-medicating and in this case the drug of choice will be that drug which gives the desired medicating effect. For instance, the opiates, like heroin and morphine, are painkillers. If one has some kind of pain, such as anxiety or despair, what better way to get rid of the pain than to take a painkiller, hence the symptomatic use of heroin. In the short term this is a good solution as it does stop the pain, is quick acting, and effective, which makes it very appealing to the Child ego state, but obviously a poor long-term solution as the pain comes back as the drug wears off.

CASE STUDY 4.4: SYMPTOMATIC DRUG USER

A woman in her late thirties has a long history of chronic marijuana use. She has her first "joint" soon after she wakes up and uses the drug at regular intervals throughout the day. If she does not use, after a day or two she starts to report symptoms of what would be seen as adulthood ADD or ADHD. She reports a lack of focus, disorganization, hyperactivity, insomnia, and so forth.

White (2010) has written elsewhere on how marijuana can be used to self-medicate ADD-like symptoms. He noted this particularly when he worked in prison, where a number of inmates reported the same kind of circumstances. The recreational marijuana user has the goal of getting stoned for the euphoria. As a result this person will use intermittently. One gets a better "high" if one has not used recently. The marijuana smoker who uses consistently throughout the day, and day after day, is not taking the drug primarily for its euphoric effects but possibly for its self-medicating effects, which in this case is to reduce the symptoms of ADD or ADHD.

As mentioned above, any drugs can be used for self-medication. Marijuana has also been noted for its positive effects on insomnia. Some people will develop a pattern of use where they have a smoke just prior to going to bed and report they sleep much better when they do. Lende *et al.* (2007) have identified a significant group of methamphetamine users who use so as to function normally and be better in control of themselves and their lives. It has also been widely documented that war veterans suffering PTSD use a variety of drugs, especially alcohol, to cope with the persistent intrusive thoughts, repetitive nightmares, and flashbacks of the traumatic events they observed. In essence they drink or drug themselves into a state where the Child ego state gets decommissioned and thus the pain goes away.

This type of drug use can be long term and involve more dangerous drug use in terms of the quantities used, because tolerance builds up. These people are at times seen as drug addicts because they repetitively use drugs. This is a false view, because if the underlying problem (e.g. depression or nightmares) is cured their interest in the drug subsides. The drug is being used to solve a problem, it is not being used in a habitual and dependent way, as the "true" drug addict does, as will be discussed next.

COUNSELING THE SYMPTOMATIC USER

Symptomatic users can often end up in drug counseling of some kind. They can seek counseling themselves and may be quite motivated to change. They can also be sent by the courts, other people, or organizations that have identified they have a drug problem. As the drug use tends to be more relentless and the need to use more obvious, this can significantly impact on their lives in terms of the four Ls. They can often present with drug-related health issues, relationship problems, financial difficulties, and legal problems. Whereas the previous four types of use have much less impact on day to day life, this type of use often has a significant damaging impact on day to day living.

As to the specific counseling of symptomatic users, the approaches are many and varied. There are a large number of alternative approaches that have been put forward over the years, from purely behavioral therapies, to cognitive behavioral therapies, to cathartic therapies of emotional release, to very introspective therapies like psychoanalysis, to approaches like Alcoholics Anonymous (AA), Narcotics Anonymous, and so on. Indeed there can be significant disagreement on what you even treat. Some say only the problem drug behavior is the focus, whereas others say the treatment focus is on the painful feelings that are being medicated away. Others, like AA, in one sense are saying you do not treat anything. The person accepts he is an addict, accepts he will always be an addict, and sets about developing a lifestyle and set of relationships that involves not using alcohol.

The counseling of drug users is a special case compared to other areas of counseling. If one is suffering depression or anxiety the Child ego state does not like that and will be highly motivated to stop. Thus the client enters the counseling process with a considerable desire to solve the problem, as depression and anxiety feel very unpleasant. The degree of success in reducing the depression or anxiety varies from case to case but the bottom line is that the client is highly motivated. The difficulty in treating drug problems is there is a reduced Child ego state investment in it. The Child ego state is the strongest part of the personality and in the long run will often get what it wants. As mentioned above, symptomatic drug use is quick and effective. If one is in pain and takes a painkiller, the pain goes away. If one suffers soul-sapping depression and finds that injecting heroin takes most of it away that makes it very appealing to the Child ego state. Drugs make people feel good and people are usually reluctant to give up such things. This means the drug user enters the counseling process with less motivation to change than the person who is suffering depression, thus making the counseling more difficult.

Indeed drug counseling has developed specific techniques to deal with this unique situation. Most books on drug and alcohol counseling, including this one, have a chapter on motivational interviewing. In books on treating depression or anxiety one does not find such chapters. Why would this be? One explanation is that the depressed client already has the basic motivation. In getting better he does not have to give up anything that feels good. There is an old saying in psychotherapy, "It is always easier to treat a tightwad than a spendthrift." This tends to sum it up well.

Having said this, the success of counseling drug users compared to non-drug-using clients varies from case to case. Some are quite successful and others are less so. With symptomatic drug users it is necessary to deal with the symptom underlying the drug use at some point. The symptom, for example anxiety, developed for a very good reason. The Child ego state will only develop such a habitual way of feeling for some very good reason. In treating the symptomatic drug user one needs to find what those reasons are and deal with them in some way. The approach to counseling the symptomatic drug user involves a two-level strategy. The counselor focuses on techniques for reducing the drug-taking behavior and also focuses on reducing the symptom which forms the motivation for using the drugs in the first place. As with the other types of drug use described above, the counselor would also be providing information about the effects of drugs and harm minimization.

Dependent drug use

This final type of drug use applies to only a small group compared to the recreational drug users, but they use up a significant amount of resources in the drug counseling profession. These people often end up in counseling at some point, often multiple times over a long period of time. They may be self-referred, or be required to enter counseling through the courts, or as a part of some kind of drug rehabilitation program. Dependent drug users can be quite motivated as often they are very unhappy and desperate people whose lives are tragic.

These people have a very strong compulsion to use the drug. This is the person who is typically seen as a drug addict or is said to have a drug addiction. They find it really, really, really hard to stop using for any significant period of time. This is a crucial point in understanding and counseling these users. Their problem is not getting off drugs but staying off drugs. In their drug-using careers there have often been multiple times when they have stopped using, but after a period of time they will again start using. This group tend to engage in the more dangerous types of drug taking and are more prone to overdose or developing significant health issues that can be life threatening. They also tend to have significant problems with the law, financial problems, and family problems. They tend to have most of the four Ls as problem areas.

At times dependent drug users will be quite despairing, desperate, and self-destructive. In one sense drugs are not the problem, instead it is the lifestyle that is the problem. The drug just happens to be the thing that shows up in their lifestyle. These individuals need to change their lifestyle, which can include their family and social life, work life, their expectations and goals about life, and so on, not just their drug-taking behavior. These are not easy things to change and take time to change. In the literature one reads discussions of what is referred to as "drug-taking careers." Whereas others have a career in sport or business, this type of drug user has a career in drugs. It is their life in this sense.

Recent research on 651 current heroin users in Australia generated the following demographics of this group of dependent drug users

(Darke *et al.* 2009; some of the figures have been averaged). These give some idea of the characteristics of the dependent heroin user.

Table 4.1 Characteristics of the depedent heroin user

Length of heroin career	10 years
Male gender	66.5%
Employed	17%
Ever been in treatment	90.5%
First age of intoxication	13.7 years
Age of first heroin use	19.7 years
Daily heroin use	80%
Ever overdosed	59%
Ever imprisoned	46%

Another interesting feature one discovers in working with these types of users is the relationship with their drug of choice. If you listen to them talk about the drug it's almost as if they are talking about a partner, as I described above. Some of them, at least, develop a relationship with the drug similar in quality to a relationship one has with a spouse. It becomes their lover, confidant, and psychological support, just as another person can be. This has important implications for the treatment of these drug users.

COUNSELING THE DEPENDENT USER

Counseling a person who has been a dependent drug user for a number of years is a difficult thing to do as the person has to change his lifestyle, not just stop taking drugs. For some however it is the lifestyle in the end that gets them to stop. There are three main ways this person will stop using for an extended period of time. First, he can grow out of it. Best, Ghufran *et al.* (2008) discusses a US treatment study involving 44,000 drug users. The average length of addiction career was 9.9 years but there is considerable variation in this, "4% of the sample reporting careers of more that 20 years and 28% reporting careers of between 1 and 5 years" (p.619). The idea of an addiction career has been around for many years since

Winick (1962) presented the idea. It involves those users who develop a pattern of chronic dependent drug use and eventually mature out of it, typically developing conventional lifestyles that include families and regular employment when they do leave their drug-using career.

Australian statistics for marijuana and heroin use in 2007 by age groups are shown in Figure 4.4.

Males recent drug use: Proportion of the population 14 years and older		
Age group	Marijuana	Heroin
14 - 19	13.1	0.5
20 - 29	25.7	0.7
30 - 39	15.9	0.4
40 - 49	11.6	40+ 0.1
50 - 59	5.4	

Figure 4.4 Changes in drug use rates over age (from Australian Institute of Health and Welfare 2007)

For these two drugs the highest rates of use occur in the twenties, followed by the thirties and then a significant drop off when the forties are reached. Regardless of any debate about the timing and patterns of such careers it is safe to say that sooner or later most dependent drug users stop using or significantly reduce their use. This often corresponds with a change in lifestyle, from the "drug addict" lifestyle to a more conventional one. One of the reasons this occurs is because they burn out. The dependent drug user lifestyle is highly charged. It involves using drugs, dangerous people, overdoses, making drug deals, lying, crime, dealing with the police, prison, prostitution, and so on.

I recall one young habitual amphetamine user reporting an incident where she was recently arrested. She was asleep with her boyfriend who was a middle-level drug dealer. She woke quite suddenly to the sight of an automatic rifle a few inches from her nose. Holding it was a member of the Tactical Response Group, specially trained police who wear full face helmets and bulletproof jackets, and are armed with automatic weapons, who enter buildings where there is a real risk of weapons being fired. She awoke to the sight of the gun and this man shouting at her to get out of bed and lie on the floor, which she did whilst also being naked in a room full of men. That is a traumatic and highly charged thing to live through. It truly does get the adrenaline flowing. Someone can live like that in the twenties and thirties but it gets a bit tiring by the time one gets to the forties and fifties.

Counseling a 22-year-old habitual heroin user and a 35-year-old similar drug user involve two quite different clinical scenarios which need to be managed differently. If other treatments are having little positive result, then it may be a matter of waiting for the drug user to grow out of the use, especially with the older drug user. The counselor is looking for the "I'm getting too old for this" type of comment. One stays alert to signs given from the client that he is psychologically ready to move on to the next stage of human development. If these occur the counselor would then reflect back the "too old" feelings to the client and almost encourage his "burn out" symptoms, taking a kind of management role so as to keep the client out of as much trouble as possible until he does finally grow out of it. The counselor works with the client to temper his excesses, presenting the idea of a more conventional lifestyle, paying particular attention to not dying or getting involved in major crime, and so forth, highlighting their age and what commonly happens to drug users of his age, that is, they start to change their drug use as they reach this new stage of psychological development in their lives.

CASE STUDY 4.5: DEPENDENT DRUG USER

A 12-year regular polydrug user whose principle drug of choice was amphetamines has been clean for eight years now. At the time of stopping she was using $300 per day of drugs. She states:

> I can recall the time like it was just yesterday. It was such a pivotal turning point in my life. I was coming down off something, I can't remember exactly what. I woke up lying in a bed alone in a filthy house. I could hear the cockroaches moving about. The amount of money I had to get each day just took too much effort. Prostitution and crime take a lot of energy. The drug kind of stopped having

the effect I used to like. I found I started to still feel alone, whereas before it stopped that in me, and I never liked injecting and always felt ashamed of doing it. If others were there I would always go into a room and inject, so others could not see me. The hallucinations and delusions were getting more and more and I felt that soon I would be mad. I kept seeing people on the side of the road who were not there. In all this I had this moment of clarity where I just knew that if I did not stop using I would die. It became very clear in my mind—it was either stop or die. I went to detox and have not used since.

This woman had given up many times before but always relapsed. This shows some interesting clinical features. First, the point at hand is how she had burnt out of the lifestyle and felt she did not have the drive or energy to keep living it. In psychological terms she had reached a new stage of development in her lifecycle. When that happens the person's psyche changes, causing a change in the behaviors exhibited in the new stage of development. In this case one of those was a change in her drug use. She stopped using in a dependent way by ceasing all drug use. She is clear she can never be a recreational drug user.

The other feature that one finds from time to time with the dependent drug user is reaching the bottom of the barrel. She wakes up in bed alone in a filthy house with cockroaches. She is aware of psychotic features beginning to get out of hand and the realization that her death is a very real possibility in the not too distant future. The report of a moment of clarity means her Adult ego state finally acknowledges this in a clear and open way. Up to that point her Child ego state would have been lying to her with all sorts of rationalizations, denials, and so forth. Combine the moment of realization of how bad her life had become with her psychology moving onto the next stage of development and the conditions for stopping are set.

Indeed such circumstances have quite a good prognosis. Should the dependent user who has grown out of it and has not used for a number of years relapse and start using often it is not long before they stop again. The main reason is that human development is cumulative, which means you cannot go backwards. Once a new stage of development has been reached one cannot revert to a previous stage, at least not for any great length of time. If the woman in Case study 4.5 starts using again she will quickly find that nothing has changed and the life of the dependent user is a most unpleasant one that requires a large amount of energy and drive to maintain. It no longer fits with her stage of development and thus the desire to get out of such a lifestyle is ever present and strong. As an example, recall how you felt and lived in your early twenties. If you started living like you did at that age again what would happen? You would tire of it quite quickly; the goals and wants you had then are different from what you have now. The psychological meaning of life now is quite different and, of course, the dependent drug user relapsing would experience the same.

Also, it can be a good prognosis if she has had a few years or even longer of no drug use, then her Child ego state knows that she can live like that. It has first-hand experience which is compelling evidence, compared to the person who has not done that or not done it for a long time. It also means she has been able to take on a more conventional lifestyle for a significant period of time. She has learned how to have a job, keep a bank account, shower and eat regularly, mow the lawn once a month, pay off a car loan, and so forth. This may seem trivial to most, but it is an important task for the person who has lived as a "junkie" and views herself as that. It involves a significant change in self-perception for her to start seeing herself as a normal citizen. These people often have a perception of self as being antisociety, or at least on the fringe of mainstream society, and that they do not fit in. In this sense they are developing a new identity, which is no small psychological task to master.

It should also be noted that the highly charged lifestyle of the dependent user is also a paradox. Whilst it is a considerable asset in the longer term for the older drug-using client to burn out, in the short term it is a definite liability. What would happen to the woman who woke up with the gun in her face, if she got a job as a waitress? If she worked five days a week for ten dollars an hour waiting on tables? Putting a little bit away each week in her bank account as she saved up for a car? She would get very bored very quickly, and they do. As I mentioned before, this group do not have too much trouble getting off drugs, they have much more difficulty staying off drugs, and one of the reasons is because conventional lifestyles are boring. They need (or are addicted to) the excitement and adrenaline that the drug-using lifestyle gives. Counselors can suggest other high-risk activities like sky diving, mountain climbing, or motor bike racing. While good therapeutic options that are worthwhile for some, they simply do not have the same impact as having a loaded, ready-to-fire gun shoved in your face, at semi-regular intervals. The need for that level of excitement is a very real and difficult problem in counseling younger dependent drug users.

The second way by which the dependent drug user can stop using is by switching the addiction. In discussing addictions Eric Berne (1972) says, "What such people need is permission to stop taking drugs, which means permission to leave their mothers and strike out for themselves, and that is what the highly successful Synanon movement provides. Where mother's injunction says "Don't leave me!" Synanon says "Stay here instead" (pp.185–186). He also says, "Curing an addict is the easiest thing in the world—*if*. All we have to do is find something that will interest him more than the thing he is addicted to. We can cure any alcoholic *if* we can find something that will interest him more than alcohol does. So far nobody has found any such thing that will work in all cases" (Berne 1957, p.215). He is suggesting the idea of switching addictions.

As one surveys the literature one finds remarkably little written on this topic. I did find one other reference to this in Vaillant and Milofsky (1982), who discuss substitute dependencies. In the field of addictions one not uncommonly hears people talk about the idea of switching addictions. Indeed there can be debate about whether it is justified for the drug counselor to merely suggest switching from one dependency to another. Regardless of the debate, the scarcity in the literature indicates a need for some discussion on the topic, especially here, where transactional analysis can easily explain it theoretically.

In this instance the goal is not to cure the addiction but for the person to switch the drug addiction to a more harmless one. As mentioned in Chapter 3, addiction is a relational process with the drug, where the drug assumes some of the personality functions of the individual, mainly their Parent and Adult ego state functions. It is possible to have the same addictive relationship to other things besides drugs and alcohol, such as an organization. In Chapter 3 Case study 3.3 showed how a prisoner developed an addictive symbiosis with the prison system. The prison took on his

Parent and Adult ego state functions, which he found difficult to live without.

Some people let their drug rehabilitation organization take the addictive role. This is what Eric Berne was referring to with Synanon, which was a prominent drug treatment organization in the United States in the 1970s and 1980s. Alcoholics Anonymous (AA) can also be like this; as an example consider some of the twelve steps in the AA system:

1. We admitted we are were powerless over alcohol—that our lives had become unmanageable.

2. Came to believe that a Power greater than ourselves could restore us to sanity.

3. Made a decision to turn our will and our lives over to the care of god as we understood him.

(Gross 2010)

In transactional analysis terms this could be seen as giving up the Parent and Adult aspects of the personality and adopting a childlike position in life. If one accepts this philosophy of the organization, then one becomes dependent on the AA system for the Parent and Adult ego states, especially around alcohol. Other features of the AA system have been highlighted, making it more liable to the process of switching addictions. Laffaye *et al.* (2008) found the more strongly a person endorsed the AA philosophy, and the more rapidly they adopted the AA practices, the more improvement there was in alcohol use problems after four years. This in itself has an addictive quality about it, as it could be seen to represent a dependent need for a "thing" that will allow them to avoid their addiction to alcohol; they are adopting a helpless child position in their relationship with AA. It should be noted that this is not meant to be a criticism of AA. I have seen AA be of considerable assistance to many problem drinkers.

In addition Kelly, Magill, and Stout (2009) note other features of AA that are seen to make it more successful. "The main benefit of AA in aiding addiction recovery may lie in its accessibility and its long-term, 'extensive', focus" (p.254). People can have exposure to the therapeutic elements on demand and self-regulate the intensity of their self-dosing for as long as they desire. AA is also free, usually available every day of the week, most importantly during high-risk periods of relapse; a close and at times intense relationship with the sponsor is also a central feature of the AA system. These features fit the criteria of a symbiotic relationship between a person and, in this case, an organization. Figure 4.5 shows the various types of addictive relationships that can exist.

It should be noted that only some users take the switching of addictions solution to drug dependency. The reasons why are yet to be articulated. Many can effectively use the AA system and not take it on as an addiction, but there is a very real possibility of doing so. Indeed any residential drug treatment program has this possibility, as the person is living in the institution that takes control of many aspects of his life and thus can take on Parent and Adult ego state functions if the individual's personality is so structured.

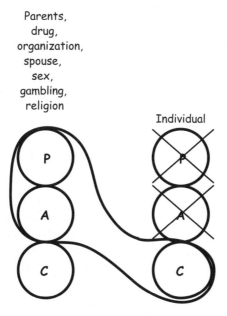

Figure 4.5 An individual can have an addictive symbiosis with a variety of different dependencies

As mentioned in Chapter 3, an addiction has two aspects: the symbiosis and an attachment. To ascertain if someone has switched their addiction from drugs to something else one would be looking for such features as:

- the desire to maintain proximity to the entity, which is a central feature in attachment, just as to another person, is in dependent personality disorder

- excessive fear or anger at the threatened withdrawal of the entity

- the entity takes on a soothing aspect for the individual

- the entity can curb some of the Free Child hedonistic excesses

- strict adherence to the rules of the entity, which can be found when one develops an addiction to a religion of some kind. Religious zealots or fundamentalists can use scriptures as their guide to life. They are seen as providing the answer on how to live, how to view the world, and what is good and bad: clear Adult and Parent ego state functions. If there is also an attachment to the system, or a teacher, or perhaps an organization involved with the particular religion, then it could be viewed to have addictive qualities similar to those found with drug addiction

- if the entity dominates the person's life, as sex and gambling addictions can. A large proportion of the person's waking life revolves around the entity, including thinking about it, talking about it, seeking it out, and so forth.

If the ex-drug user shows some of these qualities, then it is possible he has switched his addiction to something else as a way to avoid the addiction to drugs or alcohol. Some in the counseling profession are critical of such a "solution" as the addiction is not resolved (Steiner 1971). While theoretically this does have some merit, in practical terms, in my view, it is not justified. If I were an alcoholic I would much prefer to be addicted to AA than to alcohol, as I could lead a relatively normal life and not reduce my lifespan significantly. I would much prefer to be a religious fundamentalist than a heroin addict, even if they are both addictions.

However, it is true that the addiction is not resolved and as a consequence one could see the prognosis as being less favorable compared to the growing out the addiction solution. This is especially so in the early stages of no drug use, when it is quite possible for the addiction to switch back to drugs. As the time period of no use increases, the prognosis is seen to be better. Indeed, the two solutions of growing out of the addiction and switching the addiction can combine. The user may initially switch the addiction to religion or an organization. If this is maintained for a number of years the user also reaches a point where he psychologically moves onto the next stage of development and grows out of the addiction as well.

The third and final way by which the dependent drug user can stop using for extended periods of time is a derivative of the solution just discussed, switching the addiction. This is the psychological cure. While this solution is possible, it does take a significant amount of time. It begins with the user switching the addiction from the drug to the counselor. That includes a symbiosis forming at some level and the client will see the counselor as taking on the Parent and/or Adult ego state functions. In addition the client will form an attachment to the counselor, as was discussed in Chapter 3, where the dependency graph is recreated as shown in Figure 4.6.

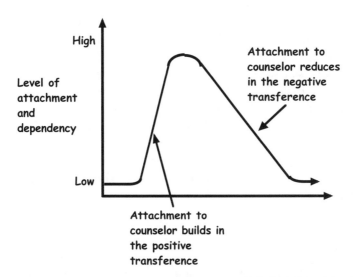

**Figure 4.6 The dependency hump and how
the transference relationship changes**

The client, in essence, moves through the process with the counselor as the attachment figure. Initially there is an increase of attachment, which is often found in what is called the positive

LIVERPOOL JOHN MOORES UNIVERSITY
LEARNING SERVICES

transference stage of therapy. At some point this switches to a negative transference and the client begins the separation process from the therapist, who is now the attachment figure in the client's mind. This was also noted by Berne (1957) who states, "This gives us a clue as to one method for attempting to cure an alcoholic: by getting him to form a more stable relationship with another person. This can sometimes be accomplished by a skillful psychotherapist who uses his influence to guide the patient into changing his behavior" (p.215).

The drug user as a child did not successfully complete the process described by the dependency hump with his original attachment figures. This leaves him with an ever-present desire for more dependency in the hope that he will again be able to finally master it. This can be done in the relationship with the counselor. If the counselor can negotiate the client through the process shown in Figure 4.6, then the constant desire for dependency reduces as the initial attachment and dependency are resolved. This then results in less of a dependency in other areas of his life, such as with drug dependency. Unfortunately this takes time, ranging from months to years, and some users respond to this better than others.

Lots of other therapeutic strategies can be used with the dependent user, some of which will be mentioned in this book, but it is the formation of a symbiosis and an attachment with the counselor that is at the basis of counseling this very problematic drug user. It must be remembered that this is only a small group of drug users; by far the largest group are the recreational users. The dependent user is often found in drug counseling, in some instances many times over a number of years, and thus they assume great importance in any statement on the machinations of drug counseling.

Conclusion

The "why" behind any drug and alcohol use is obviously of considerable importance as it directs the "how" one will treat and manage the drug user. As shown in this chapter, there are a variety of reasons why people use various drugs and not all are mutually exclusive, for instance the rebellious and dependent drug user can be one and the same, as can the symptomatic and situational drug user.

As has been described, the alternative types of use have widely different prognoses and quite varied methods of treatment. Some are relatively easy and brief, as with the experimental or recreational drug users, while others are long or difficult, as with the dependent and rebellious users.

As is sometimes the case in human functioning, it is the smallest groups that use up most of the resources, and drug counseling is no exception. By far the largest group of drug users are the recreational users and yet they rarely present for drug counseling. The smallest groups are the symptomatic and dependent users who use up most of the counseling resources. In addition, books on counseling drug users tend to focus on these two smallest groups, which this book also does, as shown in this chapter.

Part 2

Specific Techniques in Counseling the Drug and Alcohol User

Chapter 5

The Harm Reduction Contract and Harm Reduction Counseling

Introduction

Most texts on drug and alcohol counseling will include a section on harm reduction or minimization. There are a variety of issues that are addressed in the area of harm reduction. In its simplest form harm reduction counseling involves providing the client with information about the dangers involved in the consumption of drugs and how to reduce those dangers by various means.

This generally includes information regarding:

- infections—most commonly HIV and hepatitis C, what they are and how to reduce the chances of catching the virus

- overdoses—how to reduce the possibility of an overdose; what to do if someone you are with overdoses, including some basic first aid

- dangers specific to various drugs—for example, with ecstasy one must be careful the body temperature does not get too high

- mental health—the problems that can occur if one has a history or propensity for mental health problems

- dangers of injecting drug use

- not obtaining drugs on credit

- safe sex practices.

The moral issue in harm minimization

There has been a long and at times acrimonious debate about the morality of harm minimization. The abstinence school of thought says one should not teach drug users harm minimization information as it teaches them how to take drugs more comfortably and it is giving the drug user permission to take drugs.

The harm minimization school of thought says many drug-using clients are going to continue using for some time, and even if they are not currently using, they may relapse at some point. So it is better to give them the knowledge that can reduce any damage they may incur in taking drugs.

To my mind this long debate is only going to get longer because both sides are right. The harm minimization group is correct in noting that if people have such information fewer people are going to get hurt and thus it is a worthwhile task. The abstinence approach will result in more people suffering damage from taking drugs because they are less informed about the dangers. However, the abstinence view is correct in saying such information does give the drug user permission to take drugs and thus more people are going to take drugs for longer. The logic behind this can be explained quite well using transactional analysis theory.

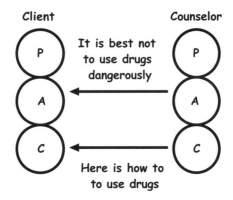

Figure 5.1 Two levels of communication in harm reduction counseling

As Figure 5.1 shows, in harm reduction counseling two pieces of information are communicated to the drug user. First, the Adult ego state information that it makes sense not to take drugs dangerously, but second, there is a Child ego state transaction. By the very act of doing harm minimization counseling the counselor is communicating that it is permissible to take drugs. This cannot be avoided, even if the counselor is very clear at the Adult level that they are not saying that. The Child ego state does not work that way. The logic behind the act of harm minimization counseling has little impact on the Child ego state, it is the actual behavior that is incorporated. As with small children, to the child part of us, behavior is much more powerful than words.

It has a similar effect to the parent who drinks alcohol and tells his son not to take ecstasy. They can provide all the logic about it being illegal and dangerous, which is all true and understood by the son, but the Child part of his personality still sees his parent taking drugs (in this case alcohol). That gives him permission to take drugs. The same applies for the counselor working with the client. They are at least tacitly giving permission to the client to use drugs if they teach harm minimization. Thus, both sides of the debate have valid points of view. It's up to the individual drug counselor to choose their moral viewpoint on this thorny issue. With harm minimization fewer people will be harmed, but permission to take drugs is given. With abstinence no permission to take drugs is given, but more people will be harmed. In harm reduction counseling it is advisable to discuss with the client the two levels of communication shown in Figure 5.1. This makes the process open and clear. In particular, discuss with the client what her Child ego state understands from this process, as that can reduce but not exclude the permission-giving aspect that comes with harm minimization.

A similar example is methadone treatment for heroin addiction. Using methadone as a treatment for heroin addiction has an inherent contradiction in it. To the Child ego state of the client it says, "Take this drug to stop taking drugs." As with harm minimization, the counselor can be clear with the client about the Adult ego state logic behind the treatment. The methadone is designed to act in such a way that the person can get her life back on track. However the Child ego state is much more influenced by behavior than by words. It simply sees it is being given another drug to take, which provides more permission to take drugs.

The difficulty of using harm minimization information

My personal choice is to engage in harm minimization counseling with clients. I will pass on information about safer drug use to clients. However there is much more to harm reduction counseling than simply passing on information. As noted by Dear (1995), knowledge of harm reduction techniques and actually using that knowledge are two different things. Some do use them, some do not use them, and some use them in varying degrees.

Dear also talks about the concept of negotiated safety. This is where the client and counselor work together and "negotiate" what harm reduction information the client is prepared to employ. The term "negotiated safety" was first coined by Susan Kippax in 1993. She looked at whether gay male couples could make explicit agreements about unprotected sex and if it had any effect on reducing the likelihood of the men having unprotected sex outside their primary relationship (Kippax *et al.* 1993). In essence the two men are negotiating about harm reduction. Research has shown this to be useful, at least to some degree. Such agreements do allow some gay men to modify dangerous sexual practices which they may have previously engaged in (Guzman *et al.* 2005; Kippax *et al.* 1997). Three studies produced the following results:

- Kippax *et al.* (1993)—81 percent had kept to the agreement after six months.

- Guzman *et al.* (2005)—61 percent had fully adhered to the agreement after three months.

- Crawford *et al.* (1998)—90 percent had behaved in a safe way, as was agreed, after six months.

This is an interesting notion, as it also relates to the idea of a no suicide contract (NSC). An NSC, as presented by White (2011), is also a harm reduction technique. The client makes a contract not to kill himself for a certain period of time. In negotiating safety with a client, the client is in essence making a contract not to harm himself. The client contracts to behave in a certain way by using harm reduction strategies. Thus the negotiation of safety and making what transactional analysis calls a contract are quite similar therapeutic procedures. Some of the features of the NSC can be employed in negotiating harm reduction techniques with a substance-using client. These will be outlined here and are discussed in much more detail in White (2011).

Ego states and negotiating safety

Any contract, including a no suicide contract or a negotiated safety contract, must be made from the Adult ego state and not the Child ego state of the client. Figures 5.2 and 5.3 show the differences in negotiating safety by an Adult ego state contract as compared to a Child ego state promise.

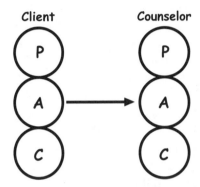

**Figure 5.2 A harm reduction contract
using the Adult ego state**

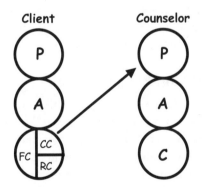

**Figure 5.3 A harm reduction promise
using the Child ego state**

A statement about future behavior (such as in negotiating safety) made from the Adult ego state is a contract. A statement about future behavior, made from the Child ego state is a promise. A contract is far more likely to be followed over time than a promise.

A contract is a statement made from the client's Adult ego state to herself about how they will behave in the future. The contract is not actually being made to the counselor, even though a counselor is often present, it is a statement by the client to self. A promise is usually made from the Conforming Child ego state to the Parent ego state of the other person.

Promises rarely work in the long run because the person is usually conforming to the orders of another. The likelihood that the person will sooner or later switch to the Rebellious Child ego state is quite high. As soon as that happens the promise will be broken. One only has to look at what happens when a child makes a promise to its mother to clean its room. First, the child does not want to do it and will only do it because its mother has demanded it. What usually happens is it either does not get done or is done resentfully in a poor manner. This is not something one wants happening when a substance-using client is negotiating about implementing harm reduction. It is incumbent on the counselor, when negotiating safety with a client, to ascertain if the person is using their Adult ego state or their Conforming Child ego state in the contracting process.

This point also highlights the problems with counseling intoxicated clients. As noted above, when a person is intoxicated her Adult ego state functioning is reduced. If she has a poorly functioning Adult ego state, she cannot make Adult ego state contracts and thus any counseling is unlikely to be effective. She certainly cannot make an effective contract whilst intoxicated.

Therapeutic relationship and negotiating safety

This incorporates what was covered in the previous section. The effectiveness of a harm reduction contract will depend partly on the nature of the relationship between the client and counselor, as do most therapeutic procedures. If the client perceives the counselor to be in an authoritarian or punitive parent type of role, then such a contract will be significantly compromised, the reason being that the client is more likely to be in the Child ego state. If a client is highly rebellious one needs to be cautious with the contracting process because it is harder to make from the Adult ego state, and she can also use the contract as a way of rebelling against the counselor.

Personal responsibility

If a client takes responsibility for her own thoughts, feelings, and behaviors she is particularly suited for a harm reduction contract. In the psychological literature this is sometimes referred to as the locus of control. An online Medical Dictionary (2011) defines the locus of control as, "A theoretical construct designed to assess a person's perceived control over his or her own behavior. The classification internal locus indicates that the person feels in control of events; external locus indicates that others are perceived to have that control." The more the person has an internal locus of control the more effective a harm reduction contract will be.

The level of personal responsibility can be assessed by simple questioning:

- Do they see their disappointments in life due to their own actions or to bad luck and timing?

- Do they believe they are in control of what they feel or are their feelings determined by the actions of others?

- Is their behavior determined by their heredity or by their choice of how to behave?

- Do they feel they are able to control their life and its outcomes or feel such things are due to fate?

Alternatively there are many simple locus of control tests which can be taken to determine if the person has an internal or external locus of control. Most of these come from the work of Rotter (1966) who developed the Rotter's Locus of Control Scale. With these factors in contracting considered one is then ready to make a harm reduction contract.

The harm reduction contracting process

The harm reduction contract (HRC) involves the client making a short statement.

> I contract with myself to stop (the potentially harmful behavior) and to (the harm reduction behavior) for "x" amount of time.

For example:

> I contract to stop sharing injecting equipment and to use only my own equipment for four days.

I contract to stop using heroin alone and to only use when there are others around me for two months.

I contract to stop having unprotected sex and to always use condoms for three weeks.

In this type of contract, as with most behavioral contracts, it is best to be quite specific about the behaviors to be stopped and started and to be specific about the day (and time if necessary) when the contract ends. When a client makes an HRC the counselor observes to see if they are displaying incongruent body language. White (2011) discusses the same idea in relation to the no suicide contract:

> Behavioral incongruities occur when where the person's behavior is incongruous with what he is saying. For example, whilst making the statement, the individual may be shaking his head as though his body language is saying "no." I have seen people cross their fingers while making such a statement, just as children do when making a promise they will not keep. One is looking for any body language that takes away from the potency of the verbalised words. Other examples may be looking down at the floor, closing one's eyes, saying the words very softly, speaking while standing on one's toes, and so on. The list is endless. As an observer it is necessary to ask oneself the question: "Does the body language appear to support what is being said, or does it make the words fragile?" (p.177)

The more congruent the body language the more solid the HRC. If the individual makes an HRC, appears to be motivated, and is in Adult ego state, then one has a good contract that can be quite effective. Obviously it is not completely foolproof, however, making a HRC is not a laborious or painful process and at best it can save a life. So it is often a worthwhile exercise to do in drug counseling.

To summarize the HRC process:

Step 1. The client and therapist discuss potentially harmful drug taking and other dangerous behavior associated with it. They negotiate what behaviors the client is prepared to alter and how. At this point the counselor may also bring up the idea of personal responsibility or assess the client to see if she has an internal or external locus of control. The more the client is willing to accept an internal locus of control the stronger the HRC.

Step 2. The client makes the HRC statement. The counselor looks for the ego state being used and any behavioral incongruencies. The client may be asked to restate the contract with different behavior if some incongruencies are observed.

Step 3. After the contract has been made the counselor discusses with the client how she will renew her contract when the time runs out. This can be done at the next session, over the phone, or with someone else who understands the process.

Step 4. The counselor asks the client what her reaction is to making the HRC.

Some report a reaction of relief. The HRC may allow them to escape a sense of being driven to hurt oneself. They may report a sense of having a part of themselves or a voice in their head that pushes them along a path of self-destruction. An HRC can allow them to escape that for a while and thus they feel relief.

At other times there may be a reaction of anxiety or fear. This is a less desirable response, where the individual may have needed their harmful behavior as a way to express the destructive part of oneself. Once that is taken away with the HRC the client is left in a state of psychological limbo wondering how she will now cope with the destructive part.

There may be little or no emotional reaction. In such cases the client may have made the statement in a parrot-like or mechanical fashion such that it has little meaning for her.

Harm reduction counseling

If one can get stoned using drugs safely or get stoned using drugs dangerously why would they ever use dangerously? This has been a question asked by many and there have been different answers over the years. Marsh and Dale (2006) report a number of these reasons:

- due to the illicit nature of some drugs

- the stereotype of the drug addict

- due to the nature of some drug-using rituals

- some are simply uninformed

- fear of rejection by fellow drug users.

These seem plausible reasons, however, in my view they miss one of the more important ones. Dear (1995) makes the following statement, "People inject drugs for a variety of reasons, and most do not want to harm themselves in the process" (p.323). I partly agree with this and partly disagree, as it depends on the type of injecting drug user.

If someone uses dangerously because she is simply unaware of the dangers, or if her dangerous use is only intermittent, then I would tend to agree with Dear that she probably does not want to harm herself. However, if a person repetitively and knowingly engages in high-risk behavior over a period of time, then that behavior is reflective of self-destructive urges. This includes any high-risk behavior such as drug use, extreme sports, driving fast cars, involvement in high-level crime, and so forth.

Psychologists have recognized for many years that repetitive patterns of behavior reflect the nature of a person's psyche. If a person has a pattern of high-risk behavior over time, then that person has some kind of desire to hurt or even kill oneself. Indeed many suicide risk assessment schedules include the question: Does the person engage in high-risk behaviors? If she does, it is seen as an indicator of elevated suicide risk.

A study by Kerr *et al.* (2009) surveyed drug users from a needle and syringe program in Melbourne, Australia. Thus they would not have been recreational heroin users but probably mostly dependent heroin users. They reported the following:

- 61 percent reported they had overdosed after injecting heroin, with the median being three times

- 84 percent reported witnessing an overdose, with the median being four-and-a-half times

- 46 percent reported witnessing an overdose in the past six months.

It is probably safe to say these figures show many of these people are living close to the edge of self-destruction. At least with dependent heroin-injecting drug users the urge unconsciously or otherwise to hurt oneself is significant and thus I would disagree with Dear (1995) about this group at least.

Self-harm and drug use

CASE STUDY 5.1: SELF-HARM

A 33-year-old female who had a long history of heroin use reports: "I used to share needles sometimes and knew it was dangerous. I knew it could hurt me or even kill me, but I think I hated myself so much I didn't really care." She had never attempted suicide and reports no suicidal urges, nor had she ever had an overdose.

This case study demonstrates one of the two ways dangerous drug use can be a reflection of the person's psyche. It can be a kind of suicide attempt or a method of self-harm (or both). Case study 5.1 indicates dangerous drug use as a means of self-harm. Her comment could indicate either suicidal urges or simply a desire to self-harm and not kill herself. To ascertain which, she was questioned about any suicidality and it was clear that she was not suicidal and never had been. Hence one can assume the dangerous injecting practices were a desire to self-harm due to a sense of self-hatred.

White (2011) notes there are eight different reasons why people will self-harm. To demonstrate the motives behind such self-harming he makes the following comment:

7. Self-harm as an expression of self-punishment or self-hatred.

Some people self-harm because of feelings of self-hatred or as a form of self-punishment. As a result of childhood experiences some end up with a self-hatred or self-loathing. This may be because they were told they were useless, worthless, not wanted, hated and loathed by the parent figures. In other circumstances the child may have been physically and sexually abused. When this happens, sometimes the child, with the magical thinking of his Little Professor ego state believes that he was abused because there is something wrong with him. It was because of his inherent badness that the parents physically abused him. The child thinks it is his fault and thus a sense of self-loathing and hatred can evolve. If a person has a basic sense of self-hatred, that does not mean they are going to be suicidal. A person will be suicidal if he has made the suicide decision and thus see[s] suicide as a viable solution to his problems. There are plenty of people who have a basic self-dislike who do not see suicide as such a solution.

Those who do have a low self-perception will self-harm in some form but maybe not in the usual sense of the word. They may not self-harm by cutting, burning, or stabbing oneself but may self-harm by the lifestyle they live. For instance a woman may prostitute herself at least partly because she hates herself. This could be seen as a type of self-harm in terms of the lifestyle she lives. Any person who has a sense of self-loathing will somehow live a lifestyle where they treat themselves badly either physically and/or psychologically. For instance, addicted drug users can take drugs in a way that amounts to physical self-harm. An example would be intravenous drug use with dirty needles with high-risk others to the extent that the user's veins eventually become mutilated. Most drug addicts also hate themselves for being addicts. They know society views a junkie as being at the lowest level of society. They are seen at least by some as the useless crap at the bottom of the pile and often view themselves in a similar light. This can amount to psychological self-harm. Thus the drug addict may hate himself and that is expressed by self-harming physically and psychologically.

There is, however, a group of self-harmers who use the more usual methods of cutting or burning as an expression of their self-hatred and self-loathing. They cut themselves as an expression of these thoughts and feelings. Some self-harmers will talk of bloodletting as a way to getting rid of their badness. As the blood flows out they see their inherent badness also flowing out. (pp.82–83)

As this quotation shows, drug use, the drug use lifestyle and dangerous drug use are easily accessible ways by which a person can self-harm. If they have self-destructive (but not suicidal) urges, these can be expressed by dangerous drug use. As mentioned above, one reaction to making an HRC is to become distressed and feel some anxiety. If a person is engaging in dangerous drug use to self-harm for the expression of self-loathing she could feel some distress at making an HRC. Her method of expressing the self-loathing is taken away by the HRC and this could leave her in an anxious state. The HRC does not remove the feelings of self-hatred, only her way of expressing it.

Counseling is needed to reduce the feelings of self-hatred, to discover why such feelings originated in the first place, and then to work through them so that they reduce. Once that happens the dangerous drug use will subside because it is no longer needed as an expression of self-hatred.

Suicide and drug use

White (2011) notes that some people make what is called the suicide decision early on in life. When confronted with adverse parenting the young child will make decisions about itself, others, and life. When a child is abused in some way at times the child can conclude that it is somehow responsible and therefore it is bad. From that the child can then conclude that it would be better for all concerned if it was not here, or can at times use its own death as payback for what it perceives as unfair treatment. This proposal has considerable support in the literature. For instance, Carr and Francis (2009) did an extensive literature review on the consequences of childhood maltreatment. They found both longitudinal and retrospective studies provided considerable evidence that trauma in childhood is associated with later adult psychopathology. In transactional analysis these are called "early decisions" and are quite similar to what cognitive behavioral therapy defines as thinking errors: erroneous conclusions the person has in her head which result in problem behavior in adulthood.

Seven such suicidal decisions have been identified:

- If you don't change I will kill myself.

- If things get too bad I will kill myself.

- I will show you even if it kills me.

- I will get you to kill me.

- I will kill myself by accident.

- I will almost die (over and over) to get you to love me.

- I will kill myself to hurt you.

(Modified from Goulding and Goulding 1979)

If an individual has urges to kill himself, a way to do it which is reasonably easy to access is with a drug overdose (with the other common one being car accidents).

CASE STUDY 5.2: *SUICIDAL BEHAVIOR*

A 30-year-old man states he has had thoughts of suicide but says he could never actually do it. He has never made a suicide attempt. Instead he describes his reckless behavior as: "It's in the bad times when all the controls I have on myself I just let go of and it's, 'I will just do what I want.' This is when my drug taking becomes reckless. Also it's in those times when I can get full of drink, get in the car and go driving recklessly." When he is in this frame of mind the intravenous amphetamine use becomes reckless and there have been a number of hospitalizations due to overdose.

This man reports he simply can never imagine himself taking his own life. He cannot imagine it in his behavioral repertoire. However, he has made a suicide decision and sees suicide as a viable solution to problems. Thus the suicide decision is to set things up so others will kill him, or to behave in high-risk ways so that a lethal "accident" eventually occurs. (White 2011, p.18)

A drug overdose is a readily available way for a drug user to carry out a suicide decision made in childhood. However, at times the line between suicide and accident can be unclear, as Case study 5.2 shows. He made the decision, "I will kill myself by accident." He also makes the statement that when times are bad his drug taking becomes reckless. If he should have a fatal overdose in one of the bad times is that a suicide or an accident? Probably a bit of both.

Dangerous drug taking is a way by which some users can live out their suicidal urges. If a person has made such a decision one way to express that decision behaviorally is to engage in dangerous drug-taking practices. Clearly in harm reduction counseling this must be taken into account. As with self-harm the counseling process is to alter the early suicide decision, and then the need to take drugs so dangerously subsides. One way to do this is with redecision therapy, which involves the client accessing the original childhood suicide decision with the help of the counselor. Once done, the counselor uses the Gestalt two-chair technique to facilitate the client accessing their Rebellious Child ego state such that they can make a redecision. This redecision involves making a new decision to live that counters the pre existing suicide decision (White 2011).

Harm reduction counseling and defence mechanisms

One further aspect to harm reduction counseling is to determine how the drug user rationalizes or defends her dangerous drug using. A person who ignores harm reduction information has to somehow rationalize away her dangerous drug taking whilst she is doing it. In essence she will need to use some kind of defence mechanism or some kind of psychological process, so that she can proceed with the dangerous and potentially fatal behavior which she is knowingly doing. Consider Case study 5.3.

CASE STUDY 5.3: DEFENSE MECHANISMS

A 37-year-old woman recalls her thinking and feeling as she ignored harm minimization information. She produced this written note in a counseling session.

Never in my wildest dreams did I ever imagine that I would share needles. Some of the details around these circumstances I can't recall. I suppose it was so traumatic, having a medical background, and a deep moral code around sharing fits, it still seems unbelievable.

I would ask the people who had used the fit before me if they had HIV or hepatitis and I chose to believe their response of "No." Truth has no place in this world, if it shows up then is gets distorted, ignored, or disproven because truth and drugs cannot be in the same room. The thought of not being able to get the drugs into me as quickly as possible, especially when watching the others getting relief from their pain was something I could not take. This anxiety...fear far outweighs the fear for my own health and life. It was like trying to resist the sound of a newborn baby crying when you're breast feeding.

I would disassociate from reality; time and space changed. I would wash the fit out with alcohol or bleach, the whole time repeating a mantra of "Please God, please God." I would think, who cares anyway, you're fucked and life is fucked and you're all fucked. Self-loathing and the fear of not getting that rush would fuel me on.

Then the ritual of mixing up would begin and my mind would start bargaining "you're not really going to do it," "you'll stop before you whack it," but there is no stopping by this stage, you're like a robot and this thing has you in its grasp. I would cry as I found a vein, wishing I could stop, jacking it back, holding in the sobs so I didn't shake too much, then pushing it down, the relief flooding over like a lover holding you in their arms no more "aghhh!!" and once again I'm clever and funny, all worries dissolve, I am a sex goddess and philosopher, brave and complete, all fears drift away.

This is a good case study as it shows a variety of psychological defences.

1. First she describes how she would ask others if they were carrying the HIV or hepatitis C virus. She knew the answer of "No" could be considered quite unreliable. To proceed she must have used some mechanism like repression or denial to push the knowledge of unreliability out of her conscious mind.

2. Next she describes how she could dissociate, which would allow her to decommission her Adult ego state temporarily, and to proceed. This may have also assisted her discounting the unreliability of her peers reporting they were virus free.

3. Then she talks about repeating the mantra, "Please God, please God." This could be the defense mechanism of magical thinking, where the Child ego state can feel safer because she has "prayed" and this will somehow magically make her safe.

4. Next she moves to an angry position with her comment, "I would think who cares anyway, you're fucked and life is fucked and you're all fucked." This may be the defense of minimization. If she can convince herself that everything is bad, then one little bit more of badness is not going to make any difference. It would allow her to minimize the importance of sharing needles.

5. Finally she talks about how her mind would start bargaining, which may be a kind of rationalization; convincing herself that her preparations for drug taking were not wrong because she will pull out at the last minute.

The number of defense mechanism techniques she used suggests she was highly motivated to do something she strongly did not want to do. It portrays a woman who was truly ambivalent about taking drugs in such circumstances. Most often there will only be one to three defense mechanisms employed. Identifying the defense mechanisms employed by the client can assist in harm reduction counseling. If the five defense mechanisms she employed did not work she would not have shared injecting equipment on that occasion. She had to explain away the dangers to herself or she would not have acted the way she did in those circumstances.

Defense mechanisms function best when they are unconscious. When the person is not aware she is using a defense mechanism is when they have the most effect. Harm reduction counseling can include working with the client to identify the defense mechanisms employed when using drugs dangerously. This can be simply done, as outlined above. The counselor writes down (or gets the client to write down) what went through her mind as she was preparing to use dangerously, as shown in Case study 5.3. The client and the counselor identify the different defense mechanisms or psychological processes used to explain away the dangers involved in the drug use.

This brings the defense mechanisms directly into the conscious Adult ego state, making it harder to successfully employ such defenses in the future. If the client wants, the counselor can keep a copy of the list in their file. I recommend doing this, as the Adult ego state of the client then knows it is down in black and white on file. This makes it harder for her to unconsciously employ similar defense mechanisms in the future. Of course, she can still use dangerously, even if she consciously knows what defense mechanisms she is currently using, but it makes it harder.

Harm minimization with youth

All of the above applies when doing harm minimization counseling with young people in their teens and early twenties. However, there is one extra consideration that must be addressed when working with youth in this way.

Adolescents are sometimes inaccurately described as being a group of risk takers. This is seen as a common attribute of the adolescent stage of development, whereas it is not actually so. Adolescents are not risk takers but are poor risk assessors. It's not that they take risks, it's that they do not see what they are doing as involving significant risk. One cannot be a risk taker if one does not see the task one is doing as risky in the first place.

An example of this is provided by Collins (1991), who discusses research about adolescent attitudes to HIV and AIDS. Although the vast majority of adolescents are knowledgeable about AIDS and its transmission, 68 percent of females and 63 percent of males had not changed their sexual behavior since learning of its possible effects. This was explained as demonstrating that adolescents believed AIDS was not their concern and instead was a problem for other people. They assumed they had a very low possibility of susceptibility and this was seen to reflect their attitude of egocentric uniqueness.

Teenagers are often described as having the attributes of egocentricity, feeling omnipotent and indestructible, of being narcissistic and of believing they have special abilities. When a teenage boy drives a car at high speed he believes he has special driving abilities, so that should he get into difficulty he has the driving skill to get himself out of trouble. He has not accurately assessed the risks involved, so in his mind he is not taking a high level of risk even though in fact he is.

CASE STUDY 5.4: *TEENAGE THINKING*

A 30-year-old recreational ecstasy user describes some of his attitudes as a teenager.

In my late teens and early twenties I was quite involved in the drug scene but I often did not practice safe sex. I would say I used a condom about 30 percent of the time. I tended to have steady girlfriends but there were times when "accidents" with other girls would happen, especially when I was drunk or stoned. Most of my girlfriends were also drug users and some of them had injected drugs in the past. I imagine some of them also had infrequent accidents with others outside our relationship.

I knew the dangers of unprotected sex and indeed of pregnancy but that did not stop me (us). I either simply didn't think about contracting HIV or some other sexually transmitted disease or I felt like somehow it would be OK and I would just be lucky. I thought I was somehow kind of special and the rules did not apply to me.

To make matters worse, before the age of 18 there were two pregnancies and both were terminated. This just provided me with more proof that if anything bad did happen I could get out of it somehow. So basically I felt I was special and indestructible.

This case study demonstrates how teenagers and young people can be poor risk assessors, which supports the research findings cited above by Collins (1991). If they do not perceive dangerous drug taking to be dangerous, or unsafe sexual practices as unsafe, then they see no need to alter their behavior. They misperceive the risk involved.

Harm reduction counseling can assess the client in this way. Does the person report a sense of omnipotence, indestructibility, or having special abilities? In essence, does the person think like a teenager? Obviously, many in adolescence will, but some adults do as well, particularly those with antisocial and narcissistic personality types. Indeed, people with these personality structures can often present with drug use issues. Harm reduction counseling with such people will allow them to examine their sense of indestructibility, specialness, egocentricity, and so forth. This can then allow them to understand that they are poor risk assessors, and how such an inability to accurately assess risk can lead to dangerous drug taking.

Conclusion

This chapter addressed the issue of harm reduction. It presented the commonly used aspects of harm reduction and also proposed some new additions such as a harm reduction contract and the analysis of defense mechanisms. Dangerous drug taking can also be reflective of urges to self-harm or be suicidal. In such instances the real problem is not the dangerous drug-taking practices but the underlying self-destructive urges.

Summary of harm reduction counseling:

- Provide harm reduction information.

- Discuss the two levels of communication given to the client during harm reduction counseling.

- Client and counselor negotiate safety, leading to a possible harm reduction contract.

- Identify any psychological motives to self-harm via drug taking.

- Identify any suicidal urges and the suicide decision.

- Identify defense mechanisms employed by the client when using drugs dangerously. Bring these into the client's Adult ego state awareness.

- Make an assessment of the client's ability to assess risk. If they "think like a teenager" in this way, counsel the client on how this can lead to dangerous drug taking.

Chapter 6

Assessment of the Drug and Alcohol User

Introduction

This chapter will provide a system by which the person seeking drug counseling can be assessed. There are many different types and forms of drug use assessment, I have developed this one over the years, drawing on others such as Helfgott (1997) and the Treatment Protocol Project (2004). This will provide the counselor with the basic information needed to make an accurate assessment of the client. The nine main areas of assessment are:

1. presenting issues
2. client history
3. drug use history
4. current drug use
5. assessment of the four Ls
6. assessing drug use and crime
7. how do they get their drugs?
8. relationships with peers and partner
9. stages of change.

From these nine areas one develops the goals of treatment as requested by the client and suggested by the counselor. In this way assessment is a collaborative process between the two people. It is done in the form of a semi-structured interview. This is preferable, as it allows the counselor to build rapport right from the beginning. It also allows the counselor to accumulate all the non-verbal communication from the client. Various charts and forms may be filled in by the client, depending on what specific assessments the counselor requires and the context of the counseling. They may include personality tests, a DSM-IV-TR diagnosis, the Beck depression inventory

(Beck 1967), and/or a myriad of other substance use rating scales, such as the Severity of Opiate Dependence Questionnaire, the Severity of Dependence Scale, and the Alcohol Use Disorders Identification test (Treatment Protocol Project 2004).

In history taking or information gathering from a client in any form of counseling one needs to be aware that the full truth is not always disclosed, at least initially. In counseling, people talk about matters that are quite personal, and about which they may be embarrassed or quite sensitive. The counselor is, of course, initially a complete stranger and thus the client may be hesitant to disclose the full story when first asked during an assessment.

While this is so in any form of counseling, it is particularly so in drug counseling. Drug use is usually an illegal activity and this in itself may result in the client being less than fully candid in the initial sessions. In addition the drug subculture is a world full of secrets and the drug scene is not a place where people do business in an honorable and transparent way.

One just needs to be aware of this, not to take it personally, and to be aware the information you get may not be the truth or the whole truth. If you are seeing the client over time, then the full story will evolve slowly as they begin to trust you more. This assessment process is therefore seen as a work in progress, that can be done over a few initial sessions, and may be modified in later sessions as more information comes to light.

Presenting issues

It seems prudent to begin an assessment by asking the client why he is here. Why has he sought counseling, how does he feel about it, and what are his current concerns? First, is he a coerced client? That is, has someone or some organization forced him to seek counseling. For example, the client may have been ordered by the courts to attend counseling, or a wife may have coerced her husband by saying that if he does not get counseling for his drinking she will divorce him. Often coerced clients will be less motivated to change their drug use than clients who are self-motivated to attend counseling.

The counselor needs to clearly identify any other party involved in the client's attendance at counseling and what their requirements are. For example, if a client was ordered to attend by the courts, does the counselor need to feed back any information to the courts about how the client was, whether he attends sessions, and so forth.

Sometimes the various parties have different motivations. The wife may want her husband to stop drinking, whereas the husband has no desire to stop drinking but does not want a divorce. It is important to clarify these factors as much as one possibly can.

Client history

This aspect of the assessment aims to gain some idea of what kind of a life the client has had from birth up until now, and the experiences he has had in a variety of areas. We are all affected by our past life experiences, in that they will influence how we behave, think, and feel in the present. As discussed in Chapter 5, Carr and Francis (2009) did an extensive literature review which concluded that a large body of literature shows association between childhood maltreatment and later psychopathology in adults. However, one needs to be careful, as there are exceptions to the rule. Some people can come from very damaged childhoods and seem to be reasonably well adjusted in adulthood. On the other hand, there are those with significant drug problems and other psychological maladjustments who appear to have had a relatively normal childhood. When the counselor has made the client history assessment he or she will have a better understanding of how past life experiences have led the client to have a drug problem now.

The usual features of a client history include:

- age, sex, contact details, and so forth
- family of origin structure
- family history
- childhood experiences
- adolescent experiences
- educational history
- occupational history
- relationship history (includes sexual history)
- financial history
- leisure pursuits history
- history of risk-taking behaviors
- history of legal issues.

Any history taking requires some caution, as it involves asking some very personal questions, including about the client's past, family relationships, childhood, and upbringing. Be sensitive to the possibility that the client may have had some painful experiences in the past that he may not wish to discuss. The client may not disclose everything during the first assessment and may hold back information. Remember you are a complete stranger (the new counselor) who is asking this person (the client) some very personal questions. If a stranger did that to you, would you be fully candid?

Drug use history

This can be represented using a time line of what drugs were used, in what amounts and at what ages (see the example in Figure 6.1).

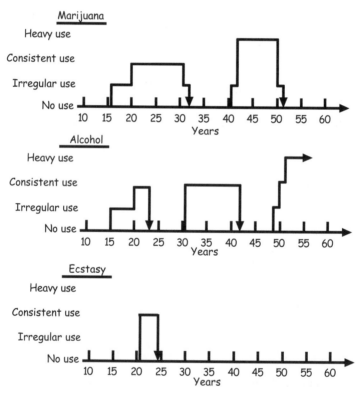

**Figure 6.1 Time line of drug use history involving
three different drugs over the lifespan**

No use is where there is no use or very intermittent use. Smoking marijuana a few times a year would be considered as no use.

Irregular use is use every couple of months or maybe short periods of regular use followed by long periods of no use. More importantly, it is not part of the person's lifestyle. He uses marijuana or cocaine if it happens to be there, so it is opportunistic use. There is little or no drive to seek the drug out, but it may be used if offered and he feels in the right mood.

An example of consistent use would be the person who is into the dance party scene and uses ecstasy there. Perhaps most weekends or a few times per month could be seen as consistent use. The drug forms part of the person's lifestyle and he is motivated to seek it out.

Heavy use would be using a number of times every week, to a level of significant intoxication. The person is motivated to seek the drug or alcohol out and it forms a significant part of his lifestyle.

This time line shows an individual who has a history of taking three different types of drugs: marijuana, alcohol, and ecstasy.

1. She began using marijuana and alcohol irregularly in her late teens.

2. Since that time her alcohol and marijuana use have tended to be mutually exclusive. When she uses marijuana she tends to not use alcohol and vice versa.

3. She currently has a pattern of heavy alcohol use and no other drug use.

4. She had a brief period of ecstasy use in her early twenties.

This time line provides an easy to understand history of the client's drug use for both the counselor and the client. Indeed, one can add more, for instance significant life events such as marriage, children, divorce, career changes, death of loved ones, and so forth. One can produce quite a detailed diagrammatic representation of the drug use in various stages of life and as related to other significant life events. I have had clients report how the visual representation of the graph has affected them afterwards, in some cases for a number of years. As they use various drugs, they at times think of the graph and where they are on it and what their graph would look like now. The client is using it as a cognitive reminder of what level of drug taking or drinking he is currently involved in. Perhaps it is the simple and clear visual nature of it that gets "stuck" in one's mind.

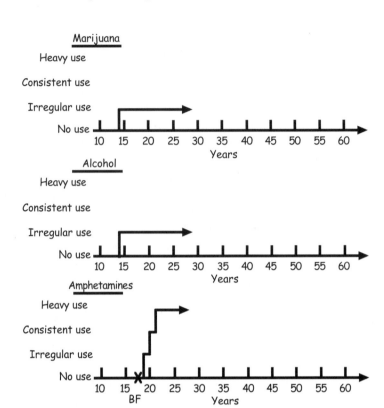

Figure 6.2 Drug use time line of a 29-year-old female

This drug use time line illustrates four prominent features.

1. Her use of marijuana and alcohol commenced about the same time, at age 14.

2. The use of marijuana and alcohol, to date, have never escalated to problem drug use.

3. Whilst being a polydrug user it is clear her drug of choice in amphetamines.

4. She began using amphetamines at age 18 and this rapidly escalated to heavy consistent use and remains so.

In this case it is important to add other life events to the time line, because she was introduced to amphetamines by a new boyfriend who she still remains in a relationship with (indicated by "BF" on the graph). This is important to note, because it's possible her use of amphetamines may alter should the relationship end. Also, as they are both dependent amphetamine users, the likelihood of one staying clean is reduced. It is very likely they would both have to stop using together and both stay clean if they are to cease their amphetamine addiction. It is very difficult for one reformed user to stay clean if they are in a relationship with another regular user.

In a drug use history it is also important to identify any:

- previous drug counseling

- involvement in other drug treatment programs such as with Alcoholic Anonymous or Narcotics Anonymous, residential treatment programs, drug programs in prison, and so forth

- what the outcomes of these treatments were in terms of periods of abstinence and relapse

- whether there has been any detoxification programs undertaken by self or with naltrexone, methadone, and so forth.

Current drug use

With the drug use history established the counselor now seeks to make an assessment of the person's current drug use. Helfgott suggests some of the following questions to ascertain this:

When does the drug use occur?

Where does it happen?

Who is it with?

What are the consequences of the use—both positive and negative?

Injecting drug use?

Polydrug use?

(Helfgott 1997, p.5)

Establish whether the drug use is:

- experimental

- rebellious

- recreational

- situational

- symptomatic

- dependent.

Assessment of the four Ls

This is often included in a drug-user assessment and provides an overview of four areas where problems are often found.

- (Liver) problems with health—what drug-related health problems there have been historically and currently

- (Lover) problems with relationships—how the drug use has impacted on relationships with friends and relatives

- (Livelihood) problems with money, housing and work—how the drug use has impacted on the person's financial position, their accommodation, and work

- (Legal) problems with the law—what drug-related legal problems there have been historically and currently. (It should be clarified that this refers only to the drug user's legal problems, not their criminal activity. There are some who have committed significant crimes and never been caught.)

Assessing drug users and crime

It is inevitable that drug counselors will counsel a significant number of clients who have spent time in prison, making it prudent to include an assessment of the drug user who has done prison time. Indeed there are many drug counselors who work in the prison system. As noted by O'Callaghan, Sonderegger, and Klag (2004): "Research has revealed a strong relationship between substance abuse and crime" (p.188). About 50 to 80 percent of inmates in Australia are in prison for drug-related offences, were drug dependent, or were drug affected at the time of the crime being committed.

People break the law and end up in prison for a variety of reasons. To ascertain the reason is productive because it affects how one would deal with the person's drug use and, indeed, manage the drug-using client over time. The framework presented here was developed from references such as the American Psychiatric Association (2000), Treatment Protocol Project (2004), consultation with others, such as

Neil McKeaig, co-worker at Acacia Prison, Western Australia (pers. comm. 2006) and my own observations in the prison system and with drug-using clients. It provides a three-group classification system.

First, there is the substance-using prisoner who fulfils the diagnostic criteria of the antisocial personality. This personality type often includes drug taking, but also has another set of personality features, such as a lack of conscience, disregard for the truth, inability to form attachments, lack of foresight, rejection of authority, and so forth (American Psychiatric Association 2000). These personality features often lead the individual into breaking the law and consequently he ends up in prison, or at least identified by the criminal justice system. If he stops taking drugs it is quite possible he will continue to be involved in criminal activity of some kind. Consequently, in counseling this type of drug user one would need to address possible reoffending and how he could avoid further drug use in prison.

The second group of prisoners who were involved with taking drugs at the time of their crime are the drug dependent users. Many of these individuals do not have an antisocial personality, but became involved in crime due to their need for drugs or because they were intoxicated at the time of the crime. When they stop taking drugs many are law-abiding citizens who are not likely to re-engage in criminal activity, and thus one does not need to address the idea of further reoffending so diligently.

The third group are those with a mental illness, such as schizophrenia. Mental health problems and substance abuse are known to co-occur in many individuals so often that it is almost the norm (Marsh and Dale 2006). These people end up in prison because they have broken the law, as a result of either their drug use or their mental illness, and not because of an antisocial personality. The following is a case study of a man I worked with in prison.

CASE STUDY 6.1: SCHIZOPHRENIA

A 30-year-old man was doing a long stretch of prison time for murder. He had a history of extensive alcohol abuse and a diagnosis of schizophrenia. When I met him in prison he presented as a pleasant and kind man who was very remorseful about his crime. His record showed no other serious convictions and only two convictions for disturbing the peace whilst under the influence, just prior to his current conviction.

He reports an increase in his paranoid delusions over a few years
as his alcohol use increased and as he became homeless. He ended up
living on the streets for about three years. He eventually stabbed to
death another homeless man who he was convinced was going to kill
him.

This case study shows a person who committed a crime, at least in part, due to his mental illness which was exacerbated by his alcohol use. When his psychotic symptoms were well managed it was very likely he would not reoffend or develop an alcohol problem. The crime was not a consequence of an antisocial personality.

When making an assessment of a drug user's legal history it is necessary to ascertain which group he falls into, as the management is quite different, as is the expected outcome of any treatment. For example, with the man in Case study 6.1, the therapeutic task is to make sure his schizophrenia is well managed by medication and support in the community, whereas treatment for the antisocial personality described above does not involve any such management. While there are antipsychotic drugs, there is no such thing as an anti-antisocial personality drug. Treatment in this case would be to deal with such things as an authority problem, the lack of foresight, the development of the skill of empathy, and so on.

For the second type, the drug dependent person, of course drug counseling is the central feature of treatment. If this person remains clean and sober, then it is quite likely he will not reoffend and will be able to establish a conventional pattern of living. With the antisocial personality there may be significant drug use issues that obviously need to be addressed, but they represent one part of the overall personality that leads to criminal activity. The non-antisocial personality drug dependent person presents a different set of clinical circumstances and thus needs to be dealt with differently. These people are usually easier to counsel because the other problematic personality features are not present and it is easier for them to develop non-offending, drug-free conventional lifestyles.

How do they get their drugs?

This is a helpful question, as it provides a variety of information about the client. However, one should note that this question in particular may bring out untruths, or at least incomplete information, when initially asked. The counselor needs to keep an open mind about the reliability of the information and expect to get more details in subsequent sessions. He is being asked about his dealer and what crime (if any) he is involved in, so the counselor should expect a less than fully candid response, at least initially.

This question can provide some good insight into their relationships in the drug subculture. Who supplies the drug and how? With the recreational user this is not so important, as he probably does not commit crime to support his drug use, whereas the heavy user may have to engage in crime of some sort to support his drug use. The counselor gets an assessment of what crime he is committing, at what level in terms of seriousness, and thus the resultant possible jail time. This can also expose the suicidal type of behavior, if the crime he is doing brings him into contact with very violent or potentially murderous people.

The heavy user would have established a number of dealers so that he can maintain a consistent supply. On the other hand a recreational user may not even know a dealer, instead there may be someone in the peer group who may have an older brother, or boyfriend, or some person who does know a dealer and can supply the drugs. If you are counseling the person in the peer group with the older brother who supplies drugs, you need to provide "harm minimization" information regarding the dangers of this, and how he could be charged with drug supply, even if he is not making any money out of it. This tends to be more the case with younger drug users.

Other drug users can be their own suppliers. This is most often the case with marijuana, where the user has a couple of plants growing at some secret venue. Knowledge of local laws on the legality of this needs to be acquired by the drug counselor. The question of how drugs are obtained and, indeed, this whole area of assessment can raise quite serious ethical (and even legal) issues. In drug counseling at times one sees clients who are or who have been involved in serious crime. The counselor needs to be cautious not to be given information that will require him or her to break confidentiality. A drug counselor is precisely that, a counselor, not a policeman, and it is not his or her role to acquire information of a crime from a client. It is important to keep that clear.

Knowledge of harm minimization

Chapter 5 discussed harm minimization in considerable detail. In any assessment of the client one would go through the various components of harm minimization listed below, noting the areas of which they have little knowledge, and rectifying that in subsequent harm minimization counseling.

The main areas of dangerous drug use are listed below:

- safer using methods, particularly for injecting drug users

- knowledge of drug effects, particularly the combination effects of heroin, cocaine, benzodiazepines, alcohol, and methadone, which are the most common drugs involved in overdoses

- knowledge of what to do with an overdose of an associate

- transmissions of blood-borne diseases, in particular HIV and hepatitis C

- knowledge of early psychotic symptoms

- safe sex practices

- not obtaining drugs on credit.

Relationships with peers and partner

This is a good prognostic indicator. At times changing drug use patterns also involve a change of peers and maybe even a partner, from fellow drug users to non-users. Making such a change in one's social and family life is a difficult thing to do for anyone, but especially a drug user. One needs to ascertain who the fellow drug users and non-drug users are in his current life. The higher the percentage of users the worse the prognosis, at least in the short term. Also, has the client ever shifted geographically as a means of getting away from his fellow drug users and what was the outcome? When the client is getting closer to giving up, geographically relocating can be quite an effective therapeutic strategy.

If the client is in a relationship where both parties use it can be instructive to find out the history of the relationship. Were they both using when they formed the relationship? Was one party using and the other party not, and thus one was introduced to the drug by the other? Sometimes they may have both been using, but one much more heavily than the other and the amount used by the second increased significantly when the relationship was formed. The worst scenario is when both parties are dependent users, they are in a long-term relationship, and they have children. Consider Case study 6.2. This was a statement made to me by a 25-year-old female who was in a relationship with another heavy amphetamine user (White 1997a).

CASE STUDY 6.2: *INJECTING DRUG USER*

> *One of the most intense, intimate things that I can do with my boyfriend is that we both go and score together, and then we come home and inject each other. The whole ritual of the thing. It is almost a spiritual thing and a real turn on.*

This is a very unfortunate situation, as the drug use has become more than just drug use; instead it forms an integral part of the relationship. It becomes part of the structure of the relationship. They get stoned together, they score together, they deal in drugs together, they scam for drugs together, they talk about drugs together. Many couples have close links, but it usually does not involve drugs. Sometimes couples can have a connection through their work. If two doctors should marry, then their work can become not just a job but part of how they view their coupling and how they structure their relationship together. Some couples can have similar strong views about politics or the environment. When this happens, again the views can become more than just political views: they become part of how the couple view their relationship together. In Case study 6.2 the same has happened. Drugs and drug use are how they both perceive themselves as a couple.

It is quite likely that for either party to give up drugs the relationship is going to have to end and for them to see very little or nothing each other. A dependent drug user is not going to give up drugs if they are relating regularly with another current drug user, let alone living with them. They have to stop being around drug users, at least for a significant amount of time, especially one they had an intimate relationship with. Hence my concern that if they are married and have children, ending a relationship is so much harder to do compared to a couple in a casual relationship. In these circumstances the relationship usually has to end to stop the drug use.

An interesting derivation of this relates to what the DSM-IV-TR calls *folie a deux*, or shared psychotic disorder. The American Psychiatric Association (2000) describes the syndrome as, "a delusion that develops in an individual who is involved in a close relationship with another person (sometimes called the 'inducer' or 'the primary case') who already has a Psychotic Disorder with prominent delusions" (p.332). A person enters a relationship and is heavily influenced by the other in some psychological way. In the case described, that involves taking on prominent delusions. The same characteristics of this syndrome can apply to substance-using behavior. A non-dependent drug-using person enters a relationship with another who uses drugs much more regularly. Over time she takes up a dependent type of drug-using pattern as she is the more passive one in the relationship, who is more influenced by the other. The prognosis for this person is better because if the relationship should end she may go back to her non-dependent using pattern. This is by no means always the case, but it is more likely than for the other person who was already a dependent user before the relationship began. The counselor needs to make an assessment of the role drugs play in the relationship with a partner, and who tends to influence who in the drug taking.

Stages of change

Finally the counselor needs to make an assessment of what stage of change the drug user is at. This is done using the stages of change model originally presented by Prochaska and DiClemente (1982). This model has five stages of change which can be represented diagrammatically, as shown in Figure 6.3.

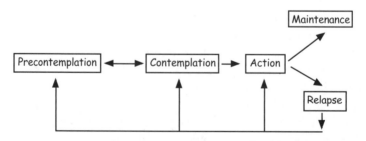

Figure 6.3 The five stages of change

Precontemplators (happy users)

These people are not worried about their drug use and give no sign of wanting to change or stop taking drugs. They do not intend to change their behavior in the near future, usually within six months. The positives of using easily outweigh the negatives and they are happy to continue using. They will ignore or minimize any information about the negatives, hazards, and so forth. These people rarely come to counseling voluntarily but can come as coerced clients.

Contemplators (unhappy users)

These people still use drugs but are beginning to worry about their use and are thinking about changing. They feel two ways about their drug taking, on the one hand it is fun and has benefits, but on the other hand it has unwanted disadvantages. They continue to gather information formally and informally about their drug use that results in more negatives being identified. Often a close associate can play a role here, if the user talks with them about their rising dissatisfactions. They can get outside encouragement to highlight the negatives. People who seek drug counseling are often at this stage. This process may eventually result in a decision being made and the individual moves onto the next stage. Alternatively, as Figure 6.3 shows, people can oscillate between precontemplation and contemplation by moving back and forth between the two.

Action

These people have changed or given up their drug use, but are in the early stages, usually less than six months. They clearly see the negatives as outweighing the positives. This is a difficult stage and these people often seek counseling. In the early stages they may feel bored, as the exciting life of the drug user is gone. They also may feel isolated, as they now avoid their drug-using friends and can feel a sense of loss as the various relationships end. Thoughts of drugs and drug use are often in the mind, but as time goes by these slowly reduce. So it's a waiting game. If they can wait long enough the new slowly becomes the old. The old habits fade away and the new habits slowly become old habits.

Maintenance

These people have changed or given up their drug use for a relatively long time, usually over six months and up to five years. The change in drug use and lifestyle has now become habitual and the norm. The thoughts about drugs are fewer, but still occur, and in some cases can occur for many years. They still need to be vigilant to avoid old associates or other triggers for drug use, but the positives of a new drug-free lifestyle are well known by now.

Relapse

As Figure 6.3 shows, the person may relapse when they are putting their decision into action and hence maintenance is not established. The decision to stop or change their use reverts to what it was before and the drug use proceeds. Indeed, one can also relapse from the maintenance stage after many years of sobriety. In this model, if someone relapses, they return to one of the earlier stages, whether that be action, contemplation, or precontemplation.

Conclusion

This chapter provided a system by which to make an assessment of a person who presents for drug counseling. Once gathered, this information allows for a thorough understanding of the client and their substance use, so that a treatment plan can be identified and employed. As mentioned previously, it may take time to get some of the information. Some of the information is quite straightforward, while other information may elicit an emotive reaction. In taking a history with clients who have suffered abuse they may recall events in their early life that are quite disturbing. They may be reluctant to mention some of these initially to the counselor. In the area of how they get their drugs there may be a resistance to being fully candid, as they may do some kind of crime in order to obtain drugs. The full story in these areas may take some time to come out completely, however as the therapeutic relationship develops, most clients will eventually disclose enough information to allow the counseling to proceed in an effective way.

Chapter 7

Drug Use Ambivalence

Introduction

Ambivalence is the state of having mixed feelings about something. So drug use ambivalence is the state of having mixed feelings about one's drug use. This is a concept that can help the drug user in a variety of ways. It allows for a better understanding of self, can be used for diagnosis, and has therapeutic uses as well. One of the difficulties in working with drug use is that you cannot see the urges or desire to use drugs. The individual may say he has strong recurrent urges to use drugs but you cannot identify the urge. This can cause difficulty, because the feelings and thoughts are not clearly defined or observable. This chapter provides a way to make the ambiguous more concrete. It provides a way of understanding drug use urges and presents them in a diagrammatic form to give a clear visual representation of what is being felt.

A great many drug and alcohol users are ambivalent about their use in varying degrees. Indeed, probably every person who uses a drug of some kind can find both positives and negatives about their use. Fortunately, with transactional analysis, this psychological state of mind can be clearly described to the individual, as shown in Figure 7.1.

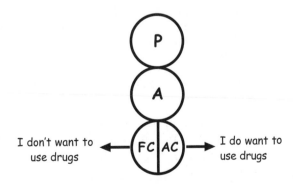

Figure 7.1 Drug use ambivalence

This diagram explains to the client how they can have two different thoughts and feelings about their drug use existing in them at the one time. Simply put, there are two different aspects of the personality that want two different things. These two parts of the personality are in conflict with each other, so at times people can feel very conflicted about their drug use. In transactional analysis theory the Adapted Child (AC) is that part of the personality that causes self-defeating behavior such as drug taking or excessive drinking. The Free Child (FC) is the part of the personality that drives the individual toward healthy behavior and hence would not want to use drugs in a harmful way. This diagram allows the counselor to describe this internal conflict to the client is a clear and simple way which facilitates the counseling process. The counselor can use it as a psychoeducational tool when necessary.

The drug use ambivalence therapeutic technique

The majority of people find this exercise a relatively simple thing to do when directed by the counselor, who can use two chairs to separate the two Child ego states. After the counselor has explained the idea of the Free Child and Adapted Child the client can be asked to experience these parts of self by sitting in two different chairs, as shown in Figure 7.2.

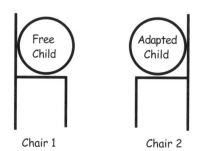

Chair 1   Chair 2

Figure 7.2 Two ego states are separated in different chairs

Two empty chairs are placed in front of the client. One chair is the FC and the other is the AC. The client sits in each chair and speaks from that part of self. First the client may sit in the AC chair and speak from the AC, he then switches and speaks from the FC ego state chair. This permits the person to actually experience those parts of self, thus allowing an experiential understanding of his drug use urges. Most people find this relatively easy to do and after a couple of times they can very easily switch into those aspects of their personality. As shown in the case studies below, the client does not sit in the FC chair and speak as he thinks the FC would, he becomes the FC aspect of his personality and talks.

CASE STUDY 7.1: *ALCOHOL USE AMBIVALENCE*

A 40-year-old male who drinks two bottles of wine each night of the week. He has done this for the past four years.

Therapist: Be the part of you that wants to drink. What does he say and feel?

Client: I like it… I like the feeling it gives me and I work hard all day and it is my present to myself at the end of the day. It's my little party with myself. All my friends don't drink or only drink a bit, they look like they are getting old.

T: Say more about that.

C: We all used to drink together but now they don't drink much at all… I have not got old like them. I like this about myself. I feel good being young in mind…but my body is getting older and that is not good for the drinking.

T: OK, that is the AC, so switch chairs and be the part that does not want to drink or drink so much.

C: Compared to others I drink a lot. Much, much more… I worry about the health effects. I have had all the blood tests and my liver and so on are fine but I worry that this will hurt me later in life. I don't like feeling like crap the next day. This gets me a bit angry at myself.

T: You feel anger at yourself?

C: Yes, when I get up in the morning feeling like shit… I get angry at me (said angrily)…each morning I promise to not drink tonight but by mid-afternoon I look forward to my little party that night. Sometimes I feel very sick but I still go to work. The odd time when I don't drink when I wake up the world looks much brighter and clearer. I am surprised by it but it shows how it effects me and I don't like it.

T: Which part is the stronger part?

C: I'm not going to stop yet…it is now 70–30 percent wanting to use. It used to be 90–10 percent wanting to use. I know if I just let myself go I will get more and more sick of it. If I try and stop myself I will only use more. I need to be very careful with the Rebellious Child in me, as that will not stop drinking if I tell it to.

This case study demonstrates the basic process of the drug use ambivalence technique. As you can see it is a quite simple and at times brief process. The client is encouraged to speak in the first person, so that he is not talking *about* the Free Child but is actually *being* the Free Child aspect of the personality. As can be seen in my initial instruction the client is invited to say what he feels. This will encourage him to move into the Child ego state and out of the Adult ego state, as the idea is to get the client to experience those aspects of the Child ego state. As a consequence in this process the client will often begin to have emotions of some kind and in Case study 7.1 it was an anger at himself. This is a good sign, as it shows he was beginning to experientially understand the Child aspect of his personality. Sometimes there is only a small amount of emotion and at other times it can be quite strong. Obviously this exercise can be repeated many times in subsequent sessions, which I often do, and usually the client quickly becomes adept at accessing those parts of the personality.

This technique provides a more comprehensive understanding of self than a purely Adult ego state understanding. The client gains a first hand experiential understanding of his desire to use drugs and his desire to not use drugs. He gets to experience what that actually feels like in a somatic and emotive way, which is a good addition to a purely intellectual understanding. In addition, the counselor gets to see all the body language that goes along with it, thus affording him or her a more comprehensive understanding of the client as compared to a simple cognitive report of the two sides of the ambivalence. The counselor gets to see where the "energy" is. If the client sits in the Free Child chair, and talks freely with animation and vigor, this shows this part of the personality is strong. If the client in the Adapted Child chair struggles to say anything, it shows there is not much investment in that part of the personality. This affords the counselor and client good insight into which is the stronger part of these two conflicted ego states at that time. Indeed, in the case example above, the counselor asks the client to rate the strength in the two ego states just experienced, again providing insight as to where this client is in relation to being ready to give up. One can repeat this exercise over time and will see the percentages change over time, thus showing how the client is progressing.

CASE STUDY 7.2: *MARIJUANA USE AMBIVALENCE*

A 29-year-old female who has smoked marijuana for many years. At times her use has been heavy but most often it is regular consistent use.

Therapist: This exercise is to let you gain an awareness of the two parts of you in relation to smoking marijuana. One part wants to smoke, and likes taking it, and the other part wants to stop or reduce your pot smoking.

So in that chair be the part that does not like smoking—tell me what she has to say? The part that wants to stop or reduce it (FC).

Client: I feel bad about it, guilt and rejected by society because of it, being hated by society because of it, alone because of it, less effective because of it, less assertive because of it, then need less people because of it too…some sort of it is me and you and let the world ease from us and we ease from them. (crying begins as she talks here)

T: What do you feel as you talk about this?

C: That I am worthless, I believe I am.

T: What do you feel?

C: Sadness.

T: Are you feeling that now?

C: Yes. (crying)

T: Experience that and say what you feel about the drug taking?

C: Just an innocent me trying to cope.

(silence)

T: OK, switch chairs and what about the part that wants to keep smoking marijuana (AC).

C: Don't feel it now.

T: OK, do you like smoking it sometimes?

C: Yes.

T: When was the last time?

C: Two days ago.

T: What did that feel like?

C: Relief, I was tired, clearing my mind.

T: Did you enjoy it?

C: Enjoy what? The smoking or the afterward? The marijuana I did not enjoy cos I was in a hurry to get home and so the afterward was good cos it numbed me. Pains go away…concerns goes away, no worries, but being in a careless moment for now.

T: What do you feel as you say this?

C: I feel like having a joint now.

T: As you look at those two parts now where do you see the energy?
Is one strong and the other not so strong?
What percentage would you put on each part?

C: I am not going to stop taking pot, so the smoking part is stronger… 90 percent.

Clearly this person is not going to stop smoking marijuana in the near future. She now understands the negative aspects of her use at an experiential level but she is quite clear and certain that she is 90 percent with the Adapted Child at this point. This is where body language is important and allows for that extra insight. When she gave the figure of 90 percent the statement was made quickly and decisively in response to my question. Her body language was congruent with her statement, allowing me to be more confident that the information given is accurate.

If she took some time to respond and the tone of voice was unconvincing, the body language would be incongruent with a figure of 90 percent, demonstrating how, by observing the Child ego state first hand, the counselor has a much more comprehensive understanding of the client. One also gets all sorts of other clinically important information as a side effect of this technique. She talks about feeling on the outside of society and that she feels worthless, which is connected to a sense of sadness. Also there is an innocent part that struggles to cope and the marijuana has the function of numbing her, thus indicating some aspect of self-medication and it being at least partly symptomatic drug use. All that comes from a simple brief technique which is designed to bring out the Child ego state.

This was the first time this woman had done this therapeutic exercise. Never before had she been asked to be and experience the two parts of her personality. Again it shows how simple and easy it is for many. There is a small group who struggle with it and find it difficult to do. Some report they are embarrassed doing it, but often if one just proceeds, within a minute they are into the technique. After it has been done, most will willingly do the exercise again, as it affords a type and level of self-understanding which is uncommon. Most people are quite interested in discovering those parts and aspects of themselves of which they were not previously aware. Perhaps it appeals to the narcissistic aspect of human nature.

From an overall therapeutic point of view it is useful as it allows the client to become more in touch with the Child aspect of their personality. For most this is a good thing, as many have become disconnected from that part of themselves to varying degrees. To experience and understand the Free Child aspect of the personality is often a psychologically healthy thing to do. Many people in modern Western societies have become out of touch with that part. The drug use ambivalence exercise is useful from this point of view as well. This does, however, identify another small group who struggle with this type of exercise and in some instances simply cannot do it: the person who is very disconnected from the Child ego state, and the person who is very parental or gets stuck in the purely intellectual Adult ego state. These people may report they just do not understand what is being asked of them. When sitting in the Child chair they simply cannot access that aspect of their personality and as a result they cannot talk from the Free Child position. Instead they remain in either their Adult or Parent ego state and it quickly becomes apparent that the exercise is not proceeding in the way it should. If this happens discontinue the technique, as it will achieve no gains in the ways described.

Conclusion

This chapter discussed the concept of drug use ambivalence; how it can provide a clear and diagrammatic way of understanding the contradictory thoughts and feelings the client may have about his drug use. This allows for more awareness and a reduction in ambiguity. Using the two chair technique the client is also afforded an experiential understanding of himself and his drug use. This is seen as a way to comprehend one's feelings and thoughts other than in a purely Adult ego state fashion. It also gives the counselor a much more comprehensive understanding of the client as he or she gets to observe first hand the client's body language relating to the two sides of the ambivalence. Using this technique over time allows the client and counselor to see whether the two sides of the ambivalence are going up or down in potency.

Chapter 8

Relapse Process Work

Introduction

Any statement on drug and alcohol counseling must include a section on relapse. Drug counselors regularly come across clients who relapse. Indeed Marsh and Dale (2006) report, "Research indicates that between 60 and 90 percent of AOD clients will reuse their problem substance within the first twelve months after treatment" (p.94). However, most books which discuss relapse will talk about relapse prevention. Presented here is a different idea, as the title of this chapter indicates. Relapse is a process. As such one does not look at relapse prevention, instead one looks at facilitating the process of relapse as a means of ending the relationship with the drug of choice. Getting off drugs is like leaving a relationship, it involves a process that one goes through.

When one leaves a significant relationship with a loved one it can be a heartbreaking process. There are many different emotions, there are good days and there are bad days, but more importantly there is a stage where the relationship is on and off, even if only in one's own mind. Couples may talk about breaking up, and in their minds psychologically withdraw from the other, or they may even break up for while. Then the relationship is reinstated, only to falter again and breaking up is again reconsidered. If they do physically move to separate homes, excuses will be made to see each other, to have a talk, to exchange goods, to talk for the sake of the children, or to hand over the dog, and so forth. In essence there is a whole series of relapses. Eventually after much turmoil and angst the couple finally do actually separate, rarely see each other again, and there are no more relapses. The couple have to go through a psychological process and that process will involve a series of relapses. Ending a significant relationship with a drug involves a similar process and that often involves a series of relapses. Relapse is an integral part of the process of ending the relationship and hence we end up with the term "relapse process work."

Of course if a relationship is of far less emotional significance, then the break up is much easier, the process is much shorter, and it involves far fewer relapses, if any at all. The same applies for one's relationship with a drug. If it's a casual one-night stand or a short intense affair, then "leaving" may involve few relapses and is a simple process. This is why one of the first and more important parts of relapse process work is to identify the nature and quality of the person's relationship with the drug.

Diagnosing the type of drug use

Chapter 4 identified differing types of drug use and the different types of relationships people can have with their drug of choice, from the casual meeting to the long-term marriage. They were as follows:

- experimental drug use
- rebellious drug use
- recreational drug use
- situational drug use
- symptomatic drug use
- dependent drug use.

How easy it is to determine the type of drug use varies. First, it requires the client to be candid, especially if the client has been coerced to attend or is perhaps a rebellious teenager. Second, if the person is, say, 35 years old one can get quite an extensive history of their drug-using patterns. If they are 15 years old one cannot determine any pattern, as they are too young for any extensive pattern to exist. However, in relapse process work the first step is to determine the type of drug use involved and construct a drug use time line, as shown in Chapter 6. Figure 8.1 shows the drug use time line of a 29-year-old female (this case was also discussed in Chapter 6, Figure 6.2).

As the client is 29 one can determine some clear patterns, as Figure 8.1 shows. She has had a casual relationship with marijuana and alcohol for 15 years (recreational drug use), and has developed a strong and intense relationship with amphetamines over the past ten years (dependent or symptomatic drug use). As with relationships between two people, the more intense and strong the relationship, the harder it is to end, and the more relapses there will probably be. If she is looking to stop her alcohol use one would expect less of a problem with relapse as compared to a decision to stop using amphetamines. This shows why it is necessary to determine the type of drug use in relapse process work.

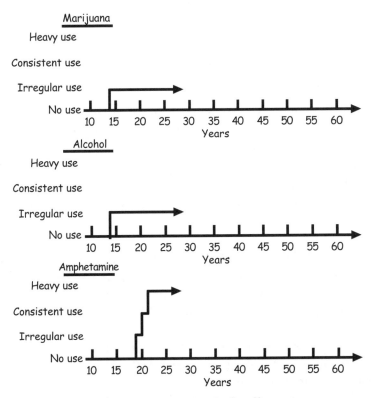

Figure 8.1 Drug use timeline

Compare this to the 15-year-old who reports smoking marijuana half a dozen times. Is this experimental use, rebellious use, recreational use, or will it develop into symptomatic use or dependent use? One does not know yet. One does know that the majority will either give up the drug altogether after not too long, or go on to recreational use, which has little negative impact on their lives. However, there is a small group of users who do go on to dependent drug use. The counselor endeavors to ascertain if the drug use is primarily a fun or a rebellious act, compared to drug use that has some more important psychological meaning. This is usually not all that difficult to determine. The counselor asks the client what she gets from the drug. After the initial statement about the high, the euphoria, and so forth one is looking for comments with more substantive meanings.

"It makes me feel clear."

"It stops the depression."

"I find I can focus."

"It removes that empty feeling in me."

"The loneliness goes away."

These types of comments indicate the drug may have a more important meaning than simply a rebellious act or a bit of fun now and then. This individual could go on to develop a dependent drug use problem, although that is by no means a certainty. She needs to be monitored and, if they agree, assisted over time, and alerted to the possibility of that type of drug use developing.

The relapse process

It is with the symptomatic and dependent drug user where the relapse counseling process is most often found. The relapse process is the process by which the person extracts herself from an important relationship, in this case with a drug. With the dependent drug user one needs to distinguish two types of relapse. As will be shown later, relapses that occur prior to the beginning of the end of the relationship with the drug have a different implication than those that occur after that point in the relationship with the drug.

As mentioned in Chapter 4, the dependent drug user has a drug-using career. The average length of career is ten years, but there is considerable variation, with some research showing about 4 percent have careers of 20 years or more and 28 percent having careers of 1 to 5 years. The point is that most dependent drug users will grow out of their addiction. They reach a time when there is significant dissatisfaction with the drug-using lifestyle and they slowly drift out of it.

Prior to this there may be periods of no use followed by a relapse. As I said previously, the problem for the dependent drug user is not getting off drugs but staying off drugs. Most will stop their drug use a number of times because it is a most unpleasant way to live life.

However, if they are not yet ready to give up, after the relapse the drug use will go back to what it was before, perhaps even more chronic. This type of relapse is different from when the point of significant dissatisfaction has been reached. This is where the relapse process occurs and the relapse process work is done. The individual slowly drifts out of the relationship, which is on and off. Slowly the "offs" (no use) become longer and the "ons" (relapse) become less intense and shorter. This can occur over many months or a number of years and is how people end all significant relationships, whether that be with another person or a drug. In this sense it is not so important if a relapse occurs, but it is the context and the meaning of the relapse that is important. Is the relapse a part of the relapse process of ending a relationship, or is it a relapse where the person is not at the point of ending their drug-using career? With the dependent drug user the counseling up to that time is designed to assist the client to reach that point of significant dissatisfaction sooner than they otherwise would. Let's look at this proposal in more detail.

The dependent drug-using career

As a quick exercise, recall a relationship you had that has now ended, that was of importance and lasted for an extended period of time, usually a number of years at least, perhaps a romantic relationship between two partners, like a marriage. As the relationship is now over there must have been difficulties. The usual pattern is that in the earlier stages of the relationship there were disagreements or expressions of dissatisfaction. These were then discussed and resolved to some extent or passed by in some way, so that the relationship resumed its previous status.

Over time the dissatisfaction continued, increasing in intensity and/or frequency. Eventually a point is reached that is the beginning of the end. One or both parties change their view of the relationship and realize that it is probable that in the long term it is over. This "beginning of the end" can often only be seen in retrospect, when one looks back at the relationship after some time. Most, however, can identify an event or a period of time where this change occurred.

The same applies for the dependent drug user. In the early to mid stages of the relationship with the drug there are periods of no use and then relapse. Each period of no use is an expression of dissatisfaction with the relationship with the drug. However, because the drug is also appealing, a relapse occurs and the relationship resumes its previous status. For most, however, there comes a point that is the beginning of the end for the relationship between the drug and the user. As mentioned above, this point can often only be identified in retrospect. At the time the user is too close to it all and does not see it. However, an outsider like a counselor may be able to identify a change in attitude that reflects the beginning of the end.

After the point of the beginning of the end, relapses change in their quality and meaning. Getting out of a psychologically strong and important relationship is a thing humans find difficult to do. It takes time and some pain. Relapses are now not only an expression of dissatisfaction with the relationship but become the psychological process by which the person extracts themselves from the relationship.

The drug counselor becomes rather like a couples counselor, but working in reverse. Instead of working with the couple to resolve their difficulties he or she works with the drug user to heighten the difficulties and cause a separation. In particular the counselor works with the no use–relapse dyads that are shown in Figure 8.2.

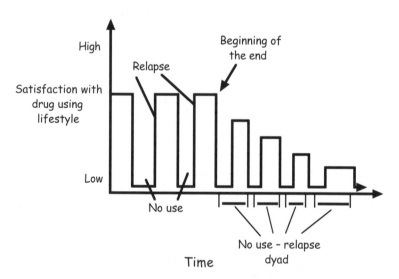

Figure 8.2 Graph of the dependent drug-using career

Initially there is a high level of satisfaction with the drug-using lifestyle. In this period there may be a number of times when the user gives up. After relapse she returns to the same level of satisfaction and the lifestyle proceeds in the same form as before. At some point this changes, and the level of satisfaction reduces to the point where the user starts to drift out of the lifestyle and drug scene. This is the beginning of the end, where the no use–relapse dyad becomes particularly important to enable the psychological extraction from the relationship. Each time a dyad is completed the drug user has less satisfaction with the lifestyle. The counselor works with the dyads, which can vary considerably in length. There may be many of them or there may only be a few. However, it is the last dyad experienced that is of most importance as this is the one that has most meaning for the user. The counselor examines with the user the last episode of no use and then relapse, what the experience was like and the impact it had on her relationship with the drug and the lifestyle. It can be compared to earlier times and dyads where there was more satisfaction with the lifestyle. A compare and contrast approach can include graphing the drug-using career as in Figure 8.2 to give the user a clear understanding of the process she is engaged in.

While the user cannot usually see the beginning of the end, the counselor is more able to, as he or she is not emotionally involved in the process. As an outside observer he or she can more easily see changes in the relationship and these can be brought to the awareness of the drug user. Most dependent drug users will spontaneously go through this process as they end their drug-using careers. Counseling can facilitate the process, potentially speeding it up and making the relapse process smoother. In addition it can assist in keeping the client alive though harm minimization and reduce the amount of negative impacts on health, legal problems, and so forth.

Of course, all concerned would prefer there to be no relapses at all. However, relapse is a common event in counseling drug users and it is generally agreed that normalizing relapse will assist in the therapeutic process (Marsh and Dale 2006). That is, raising the issue of relapse with the drug user does not encourage drug use by creating a self-fulfilling prophecy. The model presented here goes even further, saying not only that relapse is common but that in some ways it is a positive thing. The no use–relapse dyad allows the user to leave the relationship with the drug when she has reached the stage of the beginning of the end. It seems wise to be candid with the client about this, rather than withholding the information, but of course still working with her to avoid any future relapses.

Stages of change model problems

The stages of change model discussed in Chapter 6 is used extensively in drug and alcohol counseling. This discussion on relapse adds further insight into that model that can be useful in the counseling process. In particular, the model of relapse presented here highlights a problem with the usual stages of change model, as shown in Figure 8.3.

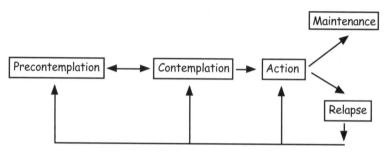

Figure 8.3 Stages of change model

In this model relapse involves the drug user going back to the beginning, or at least it is a regression. The diagram also shows relapse as a deviation away from maintenance. This does not take into account the different contexts of relapse, and their different psychological meanings. In the latter stages of the drug-using career a relapse has a positive side to it. It moves the user closer to the point of maintenance, and in that sense is not a retrograde step. It could be more accurately diagramed as shown in Figure 8.4.

The dyad of relapse and action is not a deviation from long-term maintenance but involves a move towards it, as is shown in Figure 8.4. It is how the dependent drug user gets to the point of maintenance, as that is how humans end relationships.

Geographically relocating as a therapeutic strategy

In Chapter 6 this way of dealing with problem drug use was mentioned and it is opportune to discuss it further in light of the current discussion on changing the relationship between the drug user and the drug. Geographically relocating is often done out of desperation by the drug user or close family or loved ones. Parents of a drug-dependent teenager may move her to relatives on the other side of the country or even to a different country. The rationale for this is to get her away from her drug-using peers in the hope that she can start a new life that does not include using drugs. Usually this does not work and she simply starts using in her new geographical location or finds some reason to return home and takes up where she left off.

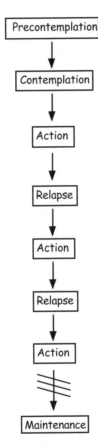

Figure 8.4 Positive aspect of relapse in the stages of change model

However, relocating is sometimes helpful. It all depends on the timing of the relocation, and the graph in Figure 8.2 provides insight into this. It can be effective if used when the drug-using career is nearing its end. If the beginning of the end has been in progress for some time, and the person is slowly drifting out of the drug scene, a geographical move can speed up the end, particularly if they are struggling with the loss of their drug-using friends and having difficulty establishing new peer relationships. If the relocation is to a supportive environment, perhaps with sympathetic relatives, then it can be quite successful, as it does give the break that is needed and a new life can be established. Timing is the key to the success, or not, of this therapeutic approach.

Relapse prevention counseling

While I have been discussing the relapse process and what to expect of the drug-dependent user, of course one wants as few relapses as possible. A common aspect of relapse prevention counseling is the idea of triggers. The counselor assists the client to identify the high-risk situations where he may use drugs again after a period of non-use. One way to do this is to simply construct a list. The exercise below shows how this can be done.

Triggers exercise

The counselor works with the client to create a list of high-risk situations. These situations can relate to feelings, thoughts, people, places, and events. Four lists are constructed to identify the triggers.

FEELINGS

Feelings can include both good and bad moods, such as:

- I got the job so I had to celebrate.
- I had a day off work.
- I get stressed out.
- I feel anxious or depressed.

THOUGHTS

The things you say to yourself that make you want to use, for example:

- I am no good and an alcoholic.
- Just one drink, that won't hurt.
- Tomorrow I will not drink for a week.

PEOPLE

People you are with who give you an increased desire to use, such as:

- When I am with my drinking friends.

- After I have seen my mother I need a drink.

- My wife nags me so much I just need to relax.

PLACES/EVENTS

Places and events where you are more likely to use:

- On Christmas Day.

- At the football.

- With a cup of coffee.

- As I sit down to watch TV at night.

Exercises such as this allow the person to identify high-risk situations. Those situations can then either be avoided altogether or prepared for in some way. This affords more protection against a relapse. Another approach is to work with the client to develop her skills at refusing offers of drink or drugs.

Drink/drug refusal skills

We live in a world where mood altering licit, illicit, and prescription drugs are widely available. One can only live in isolation for so long so as to avoid contact with these drugs. Indeed, such isolation will make one more prone to relapse as psychological deterioration ensues quickly from prolonged social isolation. Eventually the user will be offered alcoholic drinks or drugs of some kind. Developing skills at refusing such offers will also reduce the likelihood of a relapse.

SOME SKILL STRATEGIES ARE AS FOLLOWS:

Encourage the user to make a predetermined decision. If offered a drink you will answer "No." This removes the need to make an on-the-spot decision when asked the question in a social gathering. With lots going on you can say "Yes" and then have a drink in your hand before you realize what has happened.

How do you deal with subtle pressure to drink, or pressure that sometimes is not subtle at all? Role plays can be useful here. With the counselor or other group members the user can practice saying "No" and dealing with subsequent pressure. Indeed, it is educative to take both sides in the role play, being the ex-drug user answering the questions and dealing with the other pressures and also being the questioner applying pressure to the other person. Various role plays like this can be arranged, and the counselor can inquire about the feelings and the Child reactions the ex-user has to the various strategies employed by the questioner. As the reactions and feelings are defined other strategies can be discussed to cope with them should they arise in the future. Of particular importance here are the body language and assertion skills that go along with the refusal.

Not only does the ex-user need to say "No" to the person offering a drink, but, more importantly, she has to say "No" to herself. The social drinker, unlike the alcoholic, has the ability to do the transactions shown in Figure 8.5. The Child ego state has the desire for more, but the Adult ego state and the Parent ego state have the strength to curb the excesses of the Child.

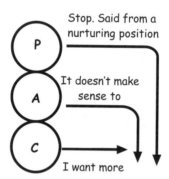

Figure 8.5 The recreational drug user and the relapse prevention transaction

The transactions illustrated in Figure 8.5 show the internal psychodynamics of the recreational drug user compared to the dependent drug user. The alcoholic or problem drug user does not have the strength in the Adult or Parent ego states to restrict the Child ego state's desire for more. The recreational drug user has these internal controls and, as a result, problem drug use never develops. From time to time one hears the problem drinker say, "When I start drinking, I just cannot stop," and she tends to keep drinking until she gets very drunk. Figure 8.5 explains what this individual is trying to describe. As mentioned earlier, alcohol decommissions the Parent and Adult ego states so that they become less influential in the decision making in the personality. This individual, whilst sober, already has poor control over the Child ego state. With the ingestion of alcohol what little control there was quickly disappears altogether, hence the person experiences a sense of being completely out of control in terms of drinking.

Figure 8.5 also shows the internal transactions used to avoid a relapse. After a period of no use there will again be a desire to relapse and use again. Indeed, for some this is a daily event, even many times a day. To avoid relapse the skills needed are strengthenings of the Adult and Nurturing Parent ego states. If they become more robust in the personality they can play more of an inhibitive effect on the Child ego state when required. The more this occurs the more the individual can avoid a relapse. This, of course, would also spill over into other areas of the person's life. She becomes more capable of living a conventional lifestyle, which the dependent drug user tends to have trouble with.

Exercising the Adult or Nurturing Parent is like exercising a muscle. The more it is used the stronger it becomes. Hence the drug user can be given a series of tasks which will exercise these two ego states. To strengthen the Adult one can do any task which requires systematic and logical thinking or decision making. That can range from mental arithmetic, to crossword puzzles, to debate that involves formulating and presenting an argument, to reading novels and the newspaper, to engaging in some kind of education. There is also significant research to show that such mental exercise can have protective effects against the development of dementia (Gatz *et al.* 2007; Lustig and Buckner 2004). This supports the assumption that it is possible to exercise the Adult ego state so that it has more influence in the personality. Indeed, in the field of dementia, there are now programs one can purchase to exercise the Adult. It seems such programs would also be useful to strengthen the Adult in order to reduce the likelihood of relapse and to increase the ability to say "No."

One can strengthen the Parent ego state in the same way, although one needs to be a bit more cautious. In the context of relapse one wants to exercise the Nurturing Parent ego state or that part of the personality that puts boundaries in place in a nurturing way, but to avoid placing boundaries in a Critical Parent way, as this will tend to encourage a Rebellious Child ego state response, which must be avoided. As shown in Figure 8.5, the recreational drinker can use her Nurturing Parent ego state to limit and control the desire by the Child ego state for more alcohol. The exercise program would involve practicing putting limitations on herself and others.

With regard to drinking, the person would have internal transactions like:

> "It's time to stop drinking now or else you will have a bad hangover tomorrow."

> "You know if you drink much more you might say some really embarrassing things which you would regret later on."

> "It's time to have a few glasses of water to take care of yourself."

One wants to avoid internal transactions such as:

> "Stop drinking now!"

> "You are looking stupid, so stop drinking!"

These are Critical Parent transactions and will tend to elicit a rebellious response, which can result in more drinking or at least more drinking in the longer term. This is particularly so for the person who uses drugs from a rebellious standpoint, as discussed in Chapter 4. One can also practice such limit setting in other areas of a person's life. For instance, one could put limitations on how much one uses the internet each day or, if one tends to stay up very late, put limits on one's own bedtime, the amount of time watching television each day, the amount of time one sleeps in, and so forth. Activities like this allow the person to exercise the limit-setting abilities of their own Child ego state.

However, this approach to relapse prevention must only be used if the person is living a somewhat hedonistic lifestyle, where the Child ego state is getting its needs and wants met excessively. This situation is particularly clear in the antisocial, hysteric, or narcissistic personalities. At times the Adult and Parent ego states are not able to control the Child ego state because its desires are so strong. To ascertain this the counselor needs to assess the level of deprivation experienced by the client.

Assessing the level of deprivation in relapse prevention

In Figure 8.5, sometimes the Child ego state want for more can be like an explosion when the person is living a very deprived lifestyle. For example, the person may be working 60 hours per week for an extended period of time, with no holidays. In these circumstances the

Child ego state is being deprived of its need for fun and its own rest and recreation. This can only go on for so long before the personality starts to break down. With extended deprivation some people may develop depression, eating disorders, panic attacks, and so forth. They can also develop an explosive drinking or drug-taking style. After all the hard work and deprivation is done, the person finally allows herself to drink or take drugs. The Child ego state likes the feeling of euphoria and so she "parties hard." She uses drugs or drinking in a gluttonous way because the Child ego state has been starved for so long. At times these drug users will say things like, "I work hard and I play hard." Sometimes these people can be functional drug users, as discussed in Chapter 4, able to use at dangerous levels but maintain a rigorous work life that not uncommonly can produce a good income.

In relapse prevention work the counselor needs to assess the extent of the Child ego state deprivation which may be occurring. The more severe it is, the more likely a relapse will occur in the future. This is usually not all that hard to assess. The counselor merely gets the client to sit in the Child ego state chair (similar to the drug use ambivalence exercise in Chapter 7), and ask what the child is feeling and thinking about life at the moment. In particular, does that part of the personality feel it is getting its wants and needs met sufficiently. Is it feeling satisfied in that way? The more satisfied it is the less likely a relapse will occur. Most do not take long to access that ego state in their personality and respond accordingly.

In terms of Figure 8.5, if there is substantial deprivation, a counselor would avoid placing more Adult and Nurturing Parent restrictions on the Child. First, he or she needs to work with the client to reduce the sense of deprivation with a change in lifestyle, so that it does get more of its needs met. Once this is achieved, then he or she can look at exercising the Adult and Nurturing Parent ego states to restrict the Child's desire for more drink and drugs.

The parts party technique in relapse prevention

This is called the parts party technique because it allows the person to experience the different parts of their personality, namely the ego states, in relation to their drug use. This technique allows the drug user and counselor to gain insight into relapse and the dynamics shown in Figure 8.5. In this process three pieces of paper are placed on the floor with Parent, Adult, and Child each written on one (or one can use three chairs). The client is then invited to stand on each piece and talk from that ego state about her thoughts and feelings of relapse and of using drugs in general. For instance, the person starts on the Child ego state piece of paper. She talks from that ego state about the desire to use and what she feels about drugs and using drugs. She then switches to the Adult ego state paper and responds to what the Child said, and then finally to the Parent ego state paper.

For example:

Child ego state: "I like drinking, it gives me a good feeling. But I drink so much it is hurting me and will kill me in the end. I have stopped for six weeks now but I feel like I will drink again. I just kind of know I will and that frightens me. I don't want to get diabetes or die but I just know deep inside me I will drink again."

Adult ego state: "I understand what you are saying and some of the feelings you express. It sounds like you are very ambivalent about your drinking. On the one hand you like the feeling of drinking and yet you also know it will harm you. I know you are quite new to all this and another strategy you could employ to help prevent a relapse is to read about the topic and learn more about the relapse process."

Nurturing Parent ego state: "I sense the pain you seem to be in and the feelings you have about a possible relapse. I care for you and will do all I can to help. You are worthwhile and deserve to live a long life."

This is where the counselor (and client) will see how effective and strong the Adult ego state is in helping to avoid a relapse. In addition the client gets to experience that part of herself first hand. She gets to feel and have a somatic understanding of that part of her personality in relation to the Child ego state and the possibility of a relapse. It also affords the counselor an opportunity to invite the client to practice their Adult responses to the Child desire to use drugs. The client can practice all sorts of Adult responses to the Child to reduce the possibility of a relapse. The counselor can also coach the client with alternative Adult ego state options, offering possible responses to make to the Child ego state. Feedback can be given to the client on how effective the response sounded and ways suggested of making the response more potent, with changes in body language, what is actually said, and so forth. The client gets to experience these with feedback provided. This is quite a potent therapeutic process to enhance relapse prevention.

The client can then move to the Nurturing Parent piece of paper and the same process is followed. At this point the counselor can also make sure the client avoids Critical Parent responses and stays with Nurturing Parent limit setting. If the client begins to slip into criticism this is brought to her attention by the counselor and she learns how to stay with Nurturing Parent and avoid Critical Parent responses to the Child ego state. The client practices in an experiential way how to respond to the Child ego state from the Nurturing Parent ego state in order to avoid relapse. As with the Adult ego state, the counselor can act as a coach, which allows the client to experiment with different types of Nurturing Parent responses whilst getting direct and immediate feedback from the counselor.

Drug use ambivalence and relapse work

The idea of drug use ambivalence, as described in Chapter 7, can be used in relapse process work and relapse prevention work. First, it can provide good insight into the current level of potential for relapse, or the client's current perception of a relapse. Consider Case study 8.1.

CASE STUDY 8.1: ASSESSING ALCOHOL RELAPSE: PART 1

A 39-year-old male, who had a chronic alcohol abuse problem for 20 years, has been clean for three years. He used Alcoholics Anonymous as the means to stop drinking. He still attends regular meetings and is actively involved with his sponsor. The idea of drug use ambivalence was described to the client and then he was asked to engage in the two-chair exercise. (It has been abbreviated just to show the main points—and some of my thinking is shown in the parentheses.)

Therapist: Be that part of you that does not want to use, and talk, what does it say?

(getting the client to talk in the first person)

Client: I have been clean and now have my family and children. I feel bad…how I hurt my children. I hit them sometimes because I was drunk.

T: OK. Be the part of you that does not want to drink and talk from it.

(I ask the same question again to encourage him to move more into his Free Child)

C: I have my life now and a home and a bank account. I have a future and have joined life how normal people live. I now have a chance to be alive…if I drink then I would die or go insane. It feels good but still unsafe.

T: Move to the other chair and be the part that does want to use and talk.

C: It does not exist. If it does exist it is just a tiny sliver. I feel my heart pumping and I am disassociating. I don't like this.

The exercise is stopped at that point and a discussion takes place. The client showed an instantaneous fear reaction to experiencing the part of himself that wants to drink, even to the point of reporting a sense of dissociation. He first said the AC part that wants to drink does not even exist. Clearly this is incongruent, because over the past few months we had openly discussed his desire to drink again and the possibility of relapse. However, it does highlight the power of this technique. He can quite easily talk from his Adult ego state about his desire to drink again, but to re-experience the Child ego state part of himself that wants to drink is a more profound experience, so his first comment, "it does not exist," is an outright refusal to even acknowledge there is a part that does want to use. It also shows how quickly people can switch ego states. In a matter of seconds they can re-experience different parts of their personality.

The strong emotional reaction indicates he is still scared of relapse and what that implies for his life. It means the AC part of him that wants to use remains a powerful part of his personality. Of course, the less the reaction, the less likely there will be a relapse, as that part has become less prominent in his overall personality structure. Hence one can make a diagnosis of how much current risk there is of a relapse and again this will wax and wane over time. Using the technique over time one can observe if the person's fear of relapse is increasing or decreasing.

As I developed this technique over time a number of colleagues, such as Lauren Fricker, psycholgist colleague (pers. comm. 2012), and indeed some clients, expressed concern about it. I had similar concerns myself. The concern was that by inviting the client to experience first hand the part of self that wants to use drugs one would be increasing the likelihood of a relapse occurring. This was a hypothesis that needed consideration, as I did not want to contribute to the possibility of a relapse. However, this was not consistent with my clinical experience, and there was some psychological theory to support the technique, such as Polster and Polster (1973). Case study 8.1, Part 1, shows a person who is unintegrated, in the Gestalt use of the term. He has, in essence, placed his AC in a box and packed it tightly away, separate from the rest of his personality. The magical thinking of the Child is, "If I can just pack it away somewhere and not notice it anymore then it stops being a danger." This, however, will lead to a sense of non-integration and theoretically makes it more dangerous in the personality. It is more likely to be expressed at some point in the future than if it was integrated.

As noted by Polster and Polster (1973), in Gestalt theory the goal is to integrate the various parts of the personality by restoring contact between the various parts of the self. The client in Case study 8.1, Part 1, had attempted to remove the AC from contact with the rest of his ego states. By inviting him to re-experience that part of himself he again begins to restore contact with the rest of his personality and thus makes the AC less formidable in the personality. The theory says that as one invites the AC into more contact with the rest of the personality it reduces its possible negative influence, which would reduce the likelihood of a later relapse.

Progressing cautiously, over time the drug use ambivalence technique was found to be of some help in relapse prevention work. As the theory hypothesized, the initial strong fear reaction quickly reduced in subsequent re-experiencing of that part of self in the chair. The second part of Case study 8.1, below, shows the response of the client, who was doing this exercise for the third time.

CASE STUDY 8.1: ASSESSING ALCOHOL RELAPSE: PART 2

T: Be the part that wants to use and talk.

C: I still get a bit of a feeling in my stomach when I do this. I want to use because its fun. I feel cheated because I cannot use just sometimes, like other people can. I want to get drunk on the weekends but I know I cannot. With me it's all or nothing. I love the feeling of being intoxicated.

T: If you had to put percentages on it what would it be?

C: It goes up and down from day to day. When I do this exercise it may go up to 20 percent wants to use, but most days it would be 10 percent want to use and 90 percent don't want to use. When I first gave up it was 99 percent want to use and 1 percent not want to use. I had cravings all the time and I used to cry myself to sleep at night. After two years it probably got to 50 percent each way.

T: With it being 99 percent at first it seems that getting yourself into a very structured detox and rehab setting was the thing you had to do.

C: Yeh... I had tried to give up by myself before and I just could not do it. I truly needed AA, the meetings, and my sponsor, and I still do.

The reactions of the client in Case study 8.1, Parts 1 and 2 are similar in quality but vary in intensity. He is getting used to the idea of experiencing the part of himself that wants to use. This is a good sign, and shows that the process of integrating it into his overall personality is progressing well and thus the likelihood of relapse is reducing. In part 1 he did not accept the AC even existed. Two sessions later he has clearly accepted that it does exist and finds it much less fearsome. Again this is a good prognostic sign for relapse prevention as the power of the AC is being reduced. As it integrates into the personality it loses its fear factor, it loses the need to repress it, and it becomes less influential in the overall personality.

The other interesting point in part 2 is the need for an intense, structured rehabilitation program when the AC was 99 percent. This client initially engaged with AA in an intense and regular way and still often attends meetings. He reports the phrase they have in AA, "Ninety meetings in ninety days," meaning that in the first 90 days of joining AA one attends 90 meetings. He also entered a highly structured, religion-based, residential drug rehabilitation center at the same time as taking on AA. With the AC being 99 percent this was the only way he was not going to relapse. If he had taken up drug counseling sessions for one hour per week on an outpatient basis it is highly likely he would have relapsed. The point being made here is that, depending on the percentage the client gives, this will determine the intensity of the treatment plan required at that point. With the AC now down to 10 or 20 percent he no longer requires a residential treatment center and he attends fewer AA meetings.

If the percentages go up, then one knows what type of treatment approach is required.

The next case study involves a 38-year-old female. She reports a history of being addicted to marijuana and amphetamines. She stopped using marijuana four years ago and has been clean from any amphetamines for three months. The drug use ambivalence concept is explained to her and she is invited to enter into the two-chair exercise about her recent amphetamine use.

CASE STUDY 8.2: ASSESSING AMPHETAMINE AND MARIJUANA RELAPSE: PART 1

Therapist: Be the part that does not want to use, what would it say?

Client: It does not say anything.

T: What does it feel like to be the part that does not want to use speed?

(there is an initial resistance so I re-ask the question to get the client into the FC ego state)

C: I got back hope when I stopped. I had lost all hope and I had good values from my parents and I could start to feel love again.

T: Yes, that is right, what else?

C: I could experience things again when I don't use. When I was using I thought I was experiencing things but when I look back now I realize I was not. I felt energy about life again.

T: Now be the part that does want to use.

C: It gave me confidence and made me more capable. I felt I could not do my study without it. All my fears and phobias would stop me from going to uni. I couldn't get dexies (dexamphetamine tablets) anymore so I started using speed instead, but you can't control it if you do that.

T: Was it also fun?

C: Yes, it was fun to use, but it was more that it made me capable and it did at first, but then it got out of control.

T: So you have the two parts. The part of you that does not want to use and the part of you that does want to use. Which is the stronger one?

C: Definitely the not want to use.

T: Would it be 80 percent don't want to use or would it be 70/30?

C: No, it would be 98 percent don't want to use.

T: What is it like to acknowledge and be that part that wants to use?

C: Scary. I want it to go away. It will get less, like the mul (marijuana) has after four years. That is 100 percent I don't want to use.

T: If someone offered you some marijuana how would you respond?

C: Definitely say no. Saying that, I do know I will use again in the future but that is years off. I have been around pot and have no interest in using. I know I am not going to use.

T: If someone offered you amphetamines now how would you respond?

C: I would still say no but I am more unsure. There is that bit that would want to say yes. It's not as sure as saying no to the pot.

As with Case study 8.1 there is an incongruence between Adult and Child ego states. She says it is 98 percent not want to use, acknowledges that it is scary, and wants it to go away. In the past few months she has been quite able to have an Adult ego state discussion about the very real possibility of relapse, but when asked to experience it, she puts the possibility of relapse at only 2 percent. This is clearly incongruent and indicates that she, like the client in Case study 8.1, lacks an integration of the AC into the personality. Indeed she even says, "I want it to go away."

The other interesting feature of this case study is it allows a comparison of two drugs. She has not used marijuana for four years and in that instance she puts the possibility of a relapse at zero percent. Her body language was consistent with this estimation and displayed no sign of fear or angst at considering the part that wants to use marijuana again. With amphetamines her estimate (2 percent wanting to use again) was inconsistent with her body language and her fear at experiencing the part that wants to use amphetamines again. One can deduce, at this juncture, that her potential for relapse is much more likely with amphetamines than with marijuana. This also highlights the need to be cautious about the percentages given by the client as a true reflection of the possibility of relapse. The body language and feelings must be consistent with the percentage given for it to be accepted as a true reflection of the possibility of relapse. When they are inconsistent it probably reflects a sense of non-integration with the part of the personality that does want to use. This is highlighted further in a subsequent session with her, Case study 8.2, Part 2.

CASE STUDY 8.2: *ASSESSING AMPHETAMINE AND*
MARIJUANA RELAPSE: PART 2

Therapist: Be the part that does not want to use.

Client: She is OK. She is just doing her stuff and being back in life again.

T: Be the part that does want to use.

C: (laughs) She is packed away in the corner...tied up and with sticky tape over her mouth.

T: Is she a bit scary?

C: She is just packed away all in the corner and she can't say anything because of the tape on her mouth. She is just mumbling away. She has lost her voice because she has been talking so much lately and she can't say any more.

T: If you could take the tape off what would she say?

C: She can't run free yet. She will one day but she can't do it now. She has said enough already.

T: Will you draw a picture?

C: I can't draw.

T: It's not a drawing test, just draw a picture of her packed away in the corner.

C: (draws picture, see Figure 8.6)

T: As you look at her what is your reaction?

C: She is scary and she needs to be tied up with the tape over her mouth. She can come out one day but not for some time. But now she is sitting in the chair tied to it with the tape.

T: Are you angry at her?

C: No, I am not angry at her. She is just a bit frightening and just needs to stay away for the moment.

T: What does she think of me?

C: She thinks, "Let's go! Let's do our stuff and move on."

T: Today if you give the percentages to the side that wants to use and the side that does not want to use, what would they be?

C: Ninety-nine percent not want to use and 1 percent wants to use.

**Figure 8.6 Drawing of Adapted Child ego state with
duct tape over her mouth and tied to a chair**

From the dialogue above it is still obvious that the part of her that wants to use is anxiety producing. Her estimate of 1 percent that does want to use is clearly inconsistent with the amount of anxiety she has about relapse. The AC is a long way from being integrated into the personality and indeed the drawing shows that. In this woman's mind that part of her is tied up in a chair and has tape over her mouth. The therapeutic goal is to eventually have her untied and in contact with the rest of the personality, further reducing the possibility of relapse. She actually says this:

> "She can't run free yet. She will one day but she can't do it now."

> "She is scary and she needs to be tied up with the tape over her mouth. She can come out one day but not for some time."

These are quite insightful comments, as she intuitively knows that to have the AC in contact with the rest of the personality is the desired state of affairs. Some therapeutic approaches do not do this. They encourage the tying up and boxing away of the AC, which leads to further non-integration of the personality which ultimately makes relapse more likely. To encourage integration of the AC defuses its potency and the various ego states learn how to coexist, which reduces the problem and makes relapse less likely.

There is another way to encourage the AC to have contact, besides inviting the client to have contact between the various parts of the personality. I made the very first step of this in Case study 8.2, Part 2 when I said to the client, "What does she think of me?" She did not answer the question and at that point I just let it go, but I will come back to it in the near future. The AC aspect of the personality is feeling alienated and alone (just look at the drawing in Figure 8.6). When people are feeling such isolation they are psychologically fragile and susceptible to emotional and physical problems developing. It can be said their physical and psychological immune systems are particularly weakened, making them more susceptible to depression, panic attacks, substance use, and so forth. What is the cure for that? Relationships.

The way to cure a sense of alienation is by forming relationships. My question about what she thinks of me is the first step in inviting a relationship with that aspect of her personality. Over time I will want to establish a dialogue between myself and the AC of this client, such that we begin to develop relational contact. When this happens she will feel less isolated and hence the potential for problems, such as relapse, will diminish. When people have a sense of being in relationships they are more psychologically healthy. I cannot stress the importance of this enough and I will use such an approach with any self-destructive person, whether they be suicidal, self-harming, or drug abusing. If the counselor can establish relational contact with the self-destructive part of the client then a major therapeutic task has been achieved.

Conclusion

As this chapter has demonstrated, relapse prevention is an important part of any drug and alcohol counseling. The usual strategies of relapse prevention include identifying triggers, explaining the stages of change model, and demystifying relapse. This chapter has sought to add to this by articulating:

How relapse varies according to the different types of drug use and different drug use timelines. Those who are rebellious or recreational users will tend to have much less trouble with relapse than the dependent drug user. The dependent drug user has developed a far stronger attachment in the relationship with the drug compared to the recreational user and hence relapse is less likely for the recreational user.

How relapse can be part of a process where the dependent drug user ends their relationship with the drug. Ending a relationship with a drug is psychologically similar to ending a relationship with a loved one. Both have a period when the relationship tends to be off and on for a period of time. Both have relapses in this way and this is part of the process of finally ending the relationship.

How relapse can have different psychological meanings in different contexts, thus highlighting a problem with the stages of change model. Relapse in the early part of the relationship with the drug has a different meaning to a relapse in the later stages of the relationship. The stages of change model does not take this into account and this chapter highlights a variation of the model to cater for this finding.

Other specific areas of covered in this chapter include how to increase ones drink/drug taking refusal skills as illustrated in the drug relapse transaction, an assessment of the level of deprivation in relapse prevention, the parts party technique in relapse prevention, and the idea of drug use ambivalence and relapse work.

Chapter 9

Motivational Interviewing

Introduction

Motivational interviewing is a fundamental drug counseling technique that is very widely used. It involves a set of procedures that are generally quite easy to use and do not take a lot of time and effort. They are basically aimed at increasing a person's desire to change his drug and alcohol use. All drug users are ambivalent to some degree. People like their drug of choice because it makes them feel good, or at least makes them feel less bad. For many, drugs are fun that give them a high and a sense of euphoria. On the other hand, drugs come at a cost financially, socially, and from a health perspective as well. Motivational interviewing is designed to resolve the ambivalence and leave the individual with a primary drive to reduce or cease his drug use.

Two types of motivational interviewing

Motivational interviewing is a set of techniques which a client can use to increase his desire or motivation to change. In drug counseling that is either to stop using or to change his drug-using patterns. The more motivation he has to alter his drug use the more likely there will be a change in his use that is sustained over an extended period of time. There are two different groups of motivational techniques, related to two different ego states in the personality (see Figure 9.1).

These types complement each other well and should be used together. The cognitive motivational interviewing techniques are usually seen as beginning with the work of Miller (1983) and involve primarily the Adult ego state. The experiential motivational interviewing techniques involve the Child ego state and include more emotional and experiential material for the client. The origins of these are harder to ascertain, as they have been mentioned in various places over time. The earliest ones appear to come from Gestalt therapy, for instance Jim Simkin (1974), who talks about the concept of organismic disgust. Through the use of motivational interviewing the Child ego state feels a sense of organismic disgust at the problem behavior and hence is more motivated to change. Subsequently McNeel (1980) talked about "heighteners." Techniques are used such that the pain in the Child ego state is heightened, thus increasing the motivation to change. More recently Saunders and Wilkinson (1990) talk about the "psychological squirm." The client's view of himself is encouraged to conflict with his behavior and this leads to negative emotions and thus more motivation to change.

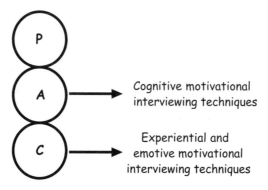

Figure 9.1 Different types of motivational interviewing

All these Child ego state techniques rest on an increase in painful feelings being experienced. Pain is one of the most basic human motivators and counselors often use this in many ways inside and outside drug counseling circles. The counselor suggests something to the client so that the Child ego state experiences some kind of painful emotion and thus he is more ready to change the behavior. Hence we have a set of techniques that involve emotion and are experiential in nature, compared to the cognitive techniques in the Adult ego state.

Cognitive motivational interviewing

What is presented here is modified from Marsh and Dale (2006), who provide a good structure for this type of motivational interviewing. Here the client is given the opportunity to weigh up the various costs and benefits of his drug use. The therapist merely writes up two lists for the client—the good things about using drugs or alcohol and the less good things about using.

1. *The good things.* It is best to start with this as the client will not be expecting it. In the past most people would have just focused on the harmful side of their drug use. In this way it can be seen to set up a non-judgmental atmosphere in the counseling.

   • Can you tell me some of the good things about using drugs or drinking?

   • What is it about using that keeps you doing it?

   Common answers are: it feels good, its fun, all my friends do it, my parents don't like it, it helps me socialize, and so forth.

   Give the client plenty of time and encouragement to come up with the good things. After they have been written down for the client the counselor can summarize them if necessary.

2. *The less good things.* Some choose not to refer to this list as the bad things because it is very negative, so often the phrase "less good things" is used.

   • We have talked about some of the good things, now tell me some of the less good things about using?

   • What are some of the not so good things about your drug use?

   Common answers are: it costs money, the hangover, it's bad for my lungs, my wife doesn't like it, the police might get me.

   Ask for some detail and remember it's the client's list, so be careful not to add your own things.

3. *Concerns.* Some counselors mistakenly assume that just because the client identifies a less good thing that means he must be concerned about it. This may not be so. The teenage marijuana smoker may mention lung cancer, but the likelihood of that is so far off into the future it is not really a concern. Or a drinker may mention money as a not so good thing but he has plenty of money to live a good lifestyle. Thus one needs to identify if the less good things are actually a concern for the client.

- Does that concern you?

- How do you feel about that?

- How much does that worry you?

Remember it is the client's concerns and not yours.

4. *Summarizing.* After both lists have been constructed the therapist summarizes both as the client looks on at the lists. The counselor may say, "It seems from these lists that some of the good things for you are…and some of the less good things for you are…?" The client is then asked for his opinion of the summary.

5. *Decision.* After the summary you may ask the client:

- Where does this leave you now?

- What does this mean for your drug use?

If the client expresses no desire to change his drug use then the counselor works on harm minimization and so forth. If he expresses some desire to change then the counselor sets about making behavior change contracts.

This type of questioning is common in the cognitive motivational interviewing approaches. As one can see it directly engages the Adult ego state to clearly describe both sides of the drug use: the side that is motivated to use and the side that is motivated to stop using. Due to its clarifying and awareness-raising properties it is best to start with this approach and then move on to the experiential motivational interviewing. Case study 9.1 is an example of cognitive motivational interviewing.

CASE STUDY 9.1: *COGNITIVE MOTIVATIONAL INTERVIEWING*

A 39-year-old female with a long history of chronic cigarette smoking.

Therapist: What are the good parts to smoking? Why do you continue?

Client: Good part. Um. It gives me time out. So when I'm at work, between classes, I get to go outside, have a wander and clear my head. I enjoy smoking. I like the way it feels as well. This is going to sound weird, but inhaling and drawing the smoke in actually feels good.

T: That's a good answer.

C: Thank you.

T: Is there anything else you can think of?

C: Not immediately off the top of my head. Um. I like the company. Smoking is a, what's the word I'm looking for, companionable happening. We stand outside, we chat, talk to new people, etc.

T: Good. OK, what are the negatives or downside to smoking?

C: Biggest one is cost. Ciggies are really expensive right now. One of the other more recent ones is the fact that people think they have the right to tell you how to quit, why you should quit, um, and that you are doing something wrong. You'd be amazed at how often people will stop you on the streets and give you the info that what you are doing is wrong.

   The other one is the health side if I get lung cancer or something.

T: I see on the packet of cigarettes you have here there is a horrible-looking picture and a slogan which says, "Smoking causes lung cancer." Is that a concern for you?

C: Usually my brain switches off the warnings and the pictures. Well, people say they are bad for me.

T: Do you think they are bad for you?

C: Probably. but I suspect my intelligence and old learning fights that. Do you know what I mean?

T: No.

C: I know enough about stats and advertising to know that what's happening is that every death of anyone who has ever smoked is probably being put down to "smoking related." Scare tactics. Also I know people who have never smoked who have died of cancer-related illnesses and I firmly believe that it is the luck of the draw. I think I've got a very strong belief that I'm going to live for a very long time.

   My friend from work, her mother quit smoking at the age of 70. She died last year at 93. Something about her has sort of done something inside me and I'm thinking 70 for quitting.

T: OK, you say the ciggies cost you money which you can't spend elsewhere. Is that a concern for you?

C: Well, they take a bit of my money but I also have plenty of money for clothes and other stuff I need.

LIVERPOOL JOHN MOORES UNIVERSITY
LEARNING SERVICES

> *T:* So it seems to me that you are clear about the good side to smoking, such as time out, you get to talk to others, and you like the sensation of inhaling. On the other hand, you seem quite aware that smoking costs you money and that ill health can result from smoking. However, these do not really concern you as it only reduces your spendable income a little bit and you seem to have a belief that you will live for a long time and the health authorities use scare tactics when announcing the statistics anyway. So this means to you?
>
> *C:* There is no way I am going to give up smoking at this time, or even try to give up smoking. But I may at a later time.
>
> *T:* OK.

As can be seen in Case study 9.1, the client was able to clearly identify the positives and negatives of smoking. The negatives are, however, of little concern to her, which means they have little motivational value and as a result her decision at this time is to continue to smoke. This case study also shows how the discussion was an Adult ego state exercise. There was no emotional expression by the client and she did not report any feelings as she was talking. It was purely a cognitive exercise, as it is meant to be. This is different to the other type of motivational interviewing which actively seeks to engage the Child ego state.

Experiential motivational interviewing

There is a variety of ways to do this type of motivational interviewing. These work less with the Adult ego state and directly engage the Child ego state, allowing the person to directly experience the feelings and somatic reactions. As a result the counselor is encouraging the client to get into his feelings and regress into the Child ego state as the exercise continues. The more this is achieved the more angst the client will feel about his drug use. If discomfort is experienced, then, as we know, that is a powerful motivator to change so as to avoid such discomfort in the future. On the other hand, this does make it a painful therapeutic technique and thus it must be used expeditiously and only when necessary.

The goal of this type of motivational interviewing is to use heighteners so as to elicit feelings of organismic disgust or psychological squirm. If the client experiences such discomfort he will have an increased motivation to do something about it and thus behavior change is more likely. One way to do this is to use the two-chair technique, as described in Chapter 7. In this case the drug is placed in the empty chair in front of the client and he is invited to respond to it in a Child ego state way. I have shown this in Case study 9.2. However, instead of using an empty chair I have used another technique. I have invited the client to draw a picture of the drug. In my office I have a large whiteboard. I get the client to draw a picture on it, then he returns to his chair and we can both easily see it. I then get the client to dialogue with the drawing so in essence we have a two-chair situation. I could have used an empty chair and asked the client to imagine the drug in the chair, but the drawing is just another way of doing the same thing.

CASE STUDY 9.2: *EXPERIENTIAL MOTIVATIONAL INTERVIEWING*

A 40-year-old male who has been drinking alcohol heavily for about ten years.

Therapist: Draw a picture of alcohol or your drinking. It can be anything. It does not have to be a bottle, or stuff, it can be anything that represents the drinking, if you like.

Client: (draws picture, see Figure 9.2)

T: Tell me about your picture.

C: It is just a large big piece of immovable concrete.

T: Say more about it.

C: That is how I feel about my drinking. I have tried so many ways to stop or cut down. Changing what I drink, using smaller glasses when I drink, organizing other activities when I would usually drink at night, drinking water every second glass, and on and on and on. But each and every time it gets back to me drinking about the same as before. It's like solid concrete that won't change.

T: What are you feeling as you say this?

(encouraging the client into feeling and the Child ego state)

C: I feel frustrated.

T: Say more about that.

(again encouraging the client to regress further)

C: It's frustrating and exasperating and feels hopeless, like I should just give up and accept the drinking that I do.

(the client is now speaking with emotion in his voice, indicating he has regressed into the Child ego state. Now is the time to use heighteners to help the client reach the point of organismic disgust)

T: Say something to the block of concrete.

C: I just look at you and see something that wont move. I can't push you. I want to shove you but you are too heavy. I think I…

(the feeling is going from the client's voice and he is becoming more Adult so I interrupt to get the client back into the regressed Child ego state)

T: Tell it what you feel about it, "I feel…"

C: I feel like you win, I give up.

T: What do you feel about that?

C: Not good and hopeless.

T: Tell it that.

C: What?

T: Tell the block of concrete that you give up and there is no hope.

(this is the heightener that is searching for the organismic disgust in the client)

C: (brief silence) I don't want that.

T: I just want you to tell the block what is real for you. You said it is hopeless, so tell it.

(another heightener)

C: (brief silence) Fuck that! No piece of concrete is going to stop me and make me give up hope.

(organismic disgust is reached such that his motivation increases to the point where he switches ego states and reacts in another way)

T: So what are you going to say to it?

C: No, not hopeless. I am not giving up.

Figure 9.2 Drawing of drinking

This case study shows that a heightener is an intervention by the counselor to heighten the discomfort in the client. In this case I got him to openly state that the situation (or "he") is hopeless. I asked him to openly state that he gives up and submits to his addiction. I asked him to openly say he gives up and lets the drug "win." Very few people will do this. Very few can say the words and when they hear them not be "disgusted," and hence motivated to do something about it. Hence we have the basis of experiential motivational interviewing.

In transactional analysis terms the goal of a heightener is to get the client to switch ego states. Initially the client was in the Conforming Child ego state. He saw the drinking as a solid block of concrete that he could never move. He was conforming to the situation that he could not stop drinking. The opposite of the Conforming Child is the Rebellious Child ego state and the role of the heightener is to assist the client to make that switch in ego states. If achieved the client changes from a passive conforming frame of mind to an active rebellious frame of mind and thus is much more likely to act on changing his drinking. At the very least he will not revert to the precontemplation stage of change and stay in the contemplator or actioner stage of change. Of course this is not the end of the story at all, however the client is now more motivated to implement changes about his drinking as he has not gone back to the precontemplator stage.

As can be seen in Case study 9.2, this must occur at a Child ego state level and I indicate in the dialogue where I have made certain interventions so as to keep the Child ego state involved.

It is necessary to initially facilitate the client regressing and then maintaining that regression throughout the exercise. A few simple rules on how to do this:

- Ask the client what he is feeling rather than what he is thinking.

- Look for any sign of the Child ego state appearing and encourage it though positive reinforcement and compliments.

- If the client starts moving into the Adult ego state, interrupt and encourage him back into feeling.

- Keep the client talking in the first person, "I feel..."

- Keep the client talking to the empty chair (or drawing in this case). If he starts talking to the counselor switch him back to talking to the chair.

- The counselor keeps his interventions short. The more words used, the more that encourages the client out of the Child ego state and more into his Adult ego state.

Motivational interviewing and the impasse

In any motivational interviewing there are three possible outcomes:

1. When the good points outweigh the not so good points the motivation is for the drug use to stay the same.

2. When the not so good points outweigh the good points the motivation is to change the drug use.

3. When the good points and not so good points are about the same weight the person is stuck at an impasse.

The concept of impasse in psychology has a long history but was particularly examined and developed as a therapeutic concept by Goulding and Goulding (1979). An impasse in counseling is reached when a client feels stuck, which can be quite a common occurrence. The individual is dissatisfied with his current behavior and thus feels motivated to change. At the same time he is not willing to adopt new behavior and thus feels motivated to stay the same. Two parts of the personality are in conflict with each other. When this occurs the goal is to heighten the sense of being stuck, which most people find frustrating and unpleasant.

CASE STUDY 9.3: *IMPASSE*

This is a later session with the same individual from Case study 9.1.

T: Put the cigarettes in the chair and talk to them. Tell them what the good side is you get from smoking?

C: What you give me is a friend, something just for me, and you help me feel less stressed.

T: Now say to the cigarettes what the downside is to smoking.

C: What I don't like is that you make me feel sick and you cost me lots of money.

T: Tell the cigarettes that you will keep smoking.

(using a heightener to achieve organismic disgust)

C: No, I don't want to do that because I waste so much money on them.

(organismic disgust is reached)

T: OK, tell the cigarettes that you will stop smoking then.

C: (silence) But I won't stop, I just know I will keep smoking.

T: So tell the cigarettes you will keep smoking for three weeks at least.

C: No, I don't want to do that.

(the client has the experience of organismic disgust and has switched ego states to the Rebellious Child, but the behavior change is not going to occur at this time. She has ended up experientially at an impasse)

T: So feel the impasse, what does it feel like? Feel it for the week.

C: I feel stuck, like in no-man's land. It's frustrating. (said with a bit of anger)

T: Feel the frustration and the sense stuckness.

(a heightener about the stuckness is being used)

C: It is yuckky…it is…frustrating…I don't like it.

T: For homework this week, experience and feel the feeling you are having now, at least once each day until our next session.

(this homework gets the client to self administer the heightener, then feel the organismic disgust, thus providing a series of ongoing motivational interviewing sessions prior to the next session)

When any client reports a sense of being stuck the counselor simply uses the same process of heightening the unpleasant experience. The counselor needs to take a step back and forget the organismic disgust about smoking cigarettes and work with the organismic disgust about being stuck at the psychological impasse. The client is invited to experience the frustration of being stuck, and, as in Case study 9.3, this will result in a sense of discomfort. For homework the client is invited to experience this discomfort at least once a day, which of course is a heightening exercise. Most will not do this for too long and will break the impasse by either going back to smoking or taking some action to change their smoking. If they go back to smoking, then the counselor uses further motivational interviewing with them at a later time.

Other factors in motivational interviewing

Before concluding, there are two other points that need to be made about motivational interviewing. First, in Case study 9.2, I stated there are very few people who will say the heightener and not feel motivated to take some kind of action. While this is a good thing, there is a small group who will not feel such motivation, not many in number, but one does come across them from time to time in counseling. Instead of feeling disgusted about giving up or feeling hopeless, they agree with it. They feel they are disgusting and hopeless.

When this happens there is significant maladjustment on behalf of the client. This person is in poor psychological condition at this time. He has what is sometimes called a characterological disorder, in the sense that Reich (1972) talks about character analysis. His basic character or sense of who he is is seen as bad, or hopeless, or worthless. He has no sense of any goodness in himself. Heighteners appeal to that spark of life in the person or that part of self that will fight and wants the best for self. While most people have this, some do not and with them such motivational interviewing must not be used as it will simply reaffirm their sense of badness.

In Case study 9.2, when asked to say to the block of concrete that he gives up and there is no hope, such damaged clients do not respond with "Fuck that! No piece of concrete is going to stop me and make me give up hope." Instead they will say "Yes, you are right, there is no hope." That is their current view of self, others, and life in general. Such heighteners in motivational interviewing will simply allow them to gain confirmation of that view. Motivational interviewing should not be used with such individuals.

Second, motivational interviewing is one of those therapeutic techniques that has an inherent contradiction. While it is used to achieve a positive psychological outcome, at the same time it can have a damaging effect on the psychology of the client, as is described below. Indeed one could say that motivational interviewing has both a good side and a not so good side. On one hand it can assist with increasing the motivation to change and on the other hand it can be emotionally abusive and damage the self-esteem of the client. This applies mainly to experiential motivational interviewing as that can facilitate a more profound sense of discomfort than cognitive motivational interviewing.

In such interviewing one of the goals is for the individual to feel organismic disgust or a sense of psychological squirm. This is obviously unpleasant, at times it can be quite unpleasant and distressing. The Australian Psychological Society (2011) presents a series of guidelines on the use of aversive therapeutic procedures. It states that there can be external aversive procedures such as the use of antabuse or electric shocks as well as internal aversive procedures such as "imagining an awful contingent event" (p.2). It seems that a procedure which produces feelings of disgust or squirming could be defined as aversive and as a result needs to be used cautiously. However, most days, counselors have to confront clients in some kind of way, and any confrontation feels unpleasant to some degree. Thus what constitutes an internal aversive procedure is a debatable point.

Despite this, the act of encouraging a person to get to a state where they feel disgust and squirm gives permission for the client to hurt self. The last thing a drug user needs is more permission to hurt self. At the very least he will model such behavior off the counselor. The counselor is modeling hurtful behavior to the drug user. Indeed the very act of doing motivational interviewing tells the client it is permissible, even good, to feel such distress. As we know, the client will introject this into his Parent ego state such that it becomes part of him. The more potent the therapeutic relationship, and the more important the counselor is to the client, the more potent the modeling will be.

Thus we are left with a conundrum. Being an aversive procedure, motivational interviewing carries an inherent contradiction, as all therapeutic aversive procedures do. It helps the client in one way and yet in another way it can harm the client. I use motivational interviewing myself, so obviously I see the positives as outweighing the negatives, at least on most occasions. However, with clients who are particularly self-destructive or who have a particularly low view of self one would use such techniques more cautiously. At the very least the contradiction in motivational interviewing needs to be brought out into the open and discussed with the client. On occasion a counselor will find a client who is using counseling partly to prove to himself that he is bad and dysfunctional, and to arrive at a point where he feels disgusted with himself actually supports the masochistic desires he has. Obviously one would need to use techniques such as motivational interviewing in a cautious fashion with such individuals.

Conclusion

Motivational interviewing is central to drug and alcohol counseling. It aims to increase motivation in the Child ego state in order to bring about change in drug-using behavior. This chapter outlined how this can be done in two different ways, first at an Adult ego state level one does what is called cognitive motivational interviewing, such that ones gains Adult awareness of one's motivational level for change. Supplementary to this is experiential motivational interviewing, which involves the Child ego state. This is less of a cognitive exercise and more of a feeling and experiential approach, such that the person gains a feeling of repulsion at taking drugs in the way they do. Both the cognitive and experiential approaches are seen to complement each other well and it is advised they be used together in the counseling process.

Sometimes in motivational interviewing the client gets stuck at an impasse. They do not want to stop taking drugs and they do want to stop taking drugs in the same degree. This, it is said, leaves the person at an impasse and this chapter discussed how to deal with impasses. Finally, this chapter identified two cautions about using motivational interviewing. First, it is inherently an aversive therapeutic procedure and thus needs to be use cautiously. Second, there is a small group of clients who do not respond well to the experiential approach and thus experiential motivational interviewing should not be used with them.

Chapter 10

The Teenage Drug User

Introduction

Any document on drug and alcohol use needs to include a special statement about the teenage drug user. This group has a quite different psychology compared to the general adult population and as a result any abnormal behavior, substance use or otherwise, is going to have different psychological mechanisms at play. These of course need to be understood, articulated, and then counseling approaches need to be modified so as to accommodate the unique features of the teenage drug user's psyche. This is no better illustrated than in Figure 10.1, compiled by Collins (1991), who did an extensive literature review and came up with a list of how experts in the field of adolescent psychology have described them.

As suffering turmoil
As being pathological
As having a marginal status
As being at a not-quite-age
As in a no-man's land
As at the way station
As the new rebel-without-a-cause
As being sexually unemployed
As being narcissistic
As being a not-quite-somebody
As being an idealist-perfectionist
As being in the learner's permit stage
As being caught in a period of rolelessness
As being disenfranchised

Figure 10.1 Features of adolescent psychology

These differentiate adolescents from the general adult population and indeed extensive research on the Minnesota Multiphasic Personality Inventory found such significant differences from the adult population that a special set of norms was produced for them (Greene 1980). The Minnesota Multiphasic Personality Inventory is a well-known and widely used personality test that identifies various aspects of the personality in the test taker. In this test it was found that adolescents are more likely to have higher elevations on the sociopathic and/or psychotic scales, similar in some respects to the criminal population (Graham 1990; Greene 1980). It should be noted however, that not all teenagers fit this profile. Graham (1990) noted that some research indicates that 25 percent of teenagers do not have profiles that differ from those of the general adult population. (That of course means that 75 percent do differ significantly.)

I have highlighted this in White 1997b and in my book *Adolescence, Anger and What to Do: A Happy Teenager is Not a Healthy Teenager* (1990b). This illustrates that this stage of development is mostly not a harmonious and balanced one. It is normal for many adolescents to be unhappy and have family relationships that are disharmonious. Sometimes parents come to me regarding relationship problems with their teenager. Whilst they are having problems they often also think they must be doing something wrong because there is disharmony in the family. I spend some time explaining that while there is disharmony, this is not necessarily abnormal, and, indeed, if there was no disquiet, then there might be something wrong. Many a parent finds this a relief.

As mentioned above, similarities have been noted between the adolescent personality and some personality features found in the criminal population. This includes characteristics such as a problem with authority, family discord, narcissism, a sense of alienation, amorality, and, at times, hyperactivity. For most, adolescence is a tough stage of life and that can include drug-taking behavior. However, in recent times this stage of development has taken on more significance because of a change in the duration of adolescence. Most modern Westernized democracies have seen a significant extension in the time period of the adolescent stage of development (Steinberg 2011; Walker 2012). This is illustrated in Figure 10.2.

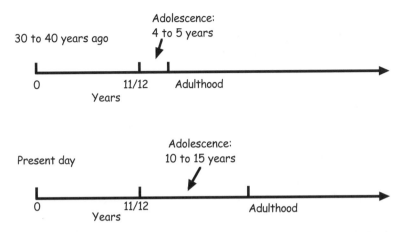

Figure 10.2 Increase in the adolescent stage of development

Why has this change occurred?

First, as a general rule, the more educated a society, the longer adolescence will be. If one is in the classroom, then one is not working. Financial independence from parents is a crucial factor for the development out of the adolescent stage and into the stage of adulthood. Also, as the lifespan increases, it is not necessary for younger teenagers to be working for society to maintain itself. The older members can take more of the workload as there are more of them available to work. Marriage is tending to occur later and so people do not have to "grow up" so early. Forty years ago marriage at 19 years of age was commonplace, nowadays it is more the exception. Related to this, childbirth is occurring later with fewer children being born in each family. This allows people to be less responsible for longer and for fewer children. In addition, societies tend to tolerate the stage of adolescence more than in the past. Antisocial teenage behavior is more accepted and the rebellious, angst-ridden teenager is considered more the norm now. And as societies become more affluent this tends to result in more "navel gazing" and adolescents, with all their foibles, allow for a lot of gazing.

It would seem that these factors have contributed to a significant increase in the duration of the adolescent stage of development. However, the main point being made here is that the counselor must change his or her thinking about the client who is a teenager. The counselor is dealing with a different kind of person compared to the adult, with significant psychological differences. In addition this group of people has now significantly increased in number due to the elongation of this developmental stage over the past 40 years.

Why teenagers use drugs

In counseling one wants to ascertain early on what the pattern of drug use has been in the past. Chapter 6 went into this in considerable detail. If one knows the past history one can get a clearer idea of what is likely to happen with future drug use. This then will determine the type of treatment one engages in with the drug user. Thus we arrive at the first difficulty with counseling the teenage drug user. One cannot ascertain the pattern of drug use. They have not used drugs or alcohol for long enough to get some idea of the type of drug use one is dealing with. As mentioned in Chapter 4 the main types of drug use are:

- experimental drug use

- rebellious drug use

- recreational drug use

- situational drug use

- symptomatic drug use

- dependent drug use.

Teenagers engage in both experimental and rebellious drug use. In Chapter 4 we saw that experimental use involves taking the drug 1 to 10 times. After that the experimenting is over, as this type of drug use is about finding out what it feels like to be intoxicated and what the drug does for them. After ten times the person is going to know how they react to the drug and if they continue to use, it is moving into another kind of drug use. Peers can also play quite a role with this type of drug use. Most often teenagers who are experimenting with, say, marijuana will do so with a friend and use together.

With rebellious use the counselor needs to identify who or what they are rebelling against. Often this is easy to do. Teenagers are often involved in rebellious use and as they move into their twenties the drug use reduces or stops, as they move out of the rebellious phase. Sometimes, however, this does not happen and the individual maintains a rebellious view and continues to use from a rebellious position for many years.

However, over time most teenagers will move on to a recreational pattern of use with drugs and alcohol, but one cannot be sure of this until a significant period of time has elapsed because a small group will go on to symptomatic and dependent use. It is in these two patterns of use where most of the damage is done and one cannot be sure if this has happened until the person has been using drugs for some time. The counselor wants to diagnose these types of drug use as early as possible and thus we have a problem in working with teenage drug users—we simply cannot do this. The majority of experimental and rebellious drug users will move on to recreational use but a small group will move on to symptomatic or dependent use.

With recreational use, the drug does not have any significant psychological meaning for the user. It is used to socialize or for fun and enjoyment every now and then. With dependent and symptomatic use the drug starts to play a significant psychological role for the user. The user can express this in a number of ways as outlined on p.148.

As mentioned earlier, some report marijuana is quite effective in treating the symptoms of ADD. Whilst intoxicated they report more ability to focus and more ability to cope with general functioning in everyday life. Teenagers who say such things could be showing some signs of a symptomatic type of drug use developing. However, one needs to be cautious in jumping to such a conclusion as teenagers can have quite significant psychological changes in a relatively short space of time. The counselor needs to be asking, "Does the drug solve a significant psychological problem for the individual?" If it does, then there is the possibility of a symptomatic drug use pattern developing.

Regarding the early signs of dependent drug use, some indicators can be found, but one needs to be careful in making such a diagnosis at this stage. One reason for this caution is that Anglin, Hser, and Grella (1997) found that, typically, dependent-type drug users first entered some kind of drug treatment 6 to 10 years after the first initiation of use, which means many will not present for drug treatment until they are well into their twenties. However, as teenagers, these individuals may end up in some type of counseling because of the lifestyle they lead, whether it be court ordered or not.

Perhaps this research shows that some of these drug users do not seriously consider giving up until six to ten years after the first use. They may indeed end up in drug counseling as teenagers but will not present their drug use as a significant problem.

One of the most common drugs used in a dependent way is heroin, followed, to a lesser extent, by cocaine. People who use heroin recreationally (i.e. not in a dependent way) over long periods present with certain characteristics. Their age of first use is relatively late. Sherwan and Dalgarno (2005) studied 126 long-term non-problematic heroin users and the average age of first use was 22.3 years. If one is counseling a 15-year-old who is using heroin, then that is one sign (only one) that it could be dependent drug use. The non-problematic heroin users typically had tried a wide variety of non-opiate drugs: cannabis (100%), ecstasy (98%), amphetamines (98%), LSD (98%), and cocaine (97%). As you can see, these are very high percentages. A teenager who is tending to use heroin exclusively is showing another possible sign of a pattern of dependent drug use. However, as one would expect, the best predictor of problem drug use developing is the teenager's close familial and social world. The more healthy attachments there are with family and friends, the less abuse there is in early life, the more they have a conventional work life, social life, and family life, and the less drug use amongst their partners, siblings, friends, and other family members, the less likely it is that dependent drug use will develop (Carr and Francis 2009; Reinhart and Edwards 2009; Rutter, Kreppner, and Sonuga-Barke 2009).

So predicting the development of a pattern of dependent drug use with a teenager is difficult to do and one must never make a "definite" diagnosis of such a young person. Adolescence is a very transitory period of life and significant psychological changes can occur during this stage of human development. However, it is worthwhile to be alert to the possibility of such a pattern developing and above I have given some of the signs one can look for.

Peers and drug use

Adolescence is the first time most young people form significant attachments outside the family, and the first time they form relationships with others not under the direct control of parents. Adolescents are also somewhat tribal in nature, they congregate in groups to hang out together. Hence the peer group for the adolescent can assume significant importance in many ways, including drug and alcohol use. Although parents sometimes like to think that their teenage boy is taking drugs because he has fallen in with a bad crowd, in the majority of cases peer groups and peer relationships are bi-directional in nature. Their "good" teenage boy is probably contributing to the "bad" behavior of other teenagers in his peer group. He is affecting their behavior as much as others are affecting his.

There are some adolescents (and adults for that matter) who are highly dependent and passive individuals, and are significantly influenced by the ideas and wishes of others. However, this is a small group and most adolescents are quite capable of making their own decisions, even if there is peer pressure to take drugs that they may not wish to take. Despite this, any member of a peer group (passive/dependent or otherwise) who smokes marijuana gives permission to the other members to also smoke marijuana. It says to the others looking on, "In our group this is the thing to do." All peer group members influence the drug-taking behavior of the others involved in the tribe. Hence the bi-directional nature of influence in peer group behavior.

Often a young person's drug use is erratic, as it takes time to make the necessary connections in the drug subculture. To make friendships in that subculture takes time. Changing a lifestyle takes some time to achieve. Most flirt with it for a while during their experimental and rebellious drug use periods and never get significantly involved. They find it is just not for them and peer groups change around this time. Those who use regularly will slowly become surrounded by peers who also use regularly and those who do not use or use very little will drift off and find similar peers of their own. A person who is intoxicated and a person who is not intoxicated cannot really socialize for all that long. The non-intoxicated person usually gets bored quite quickly and ends up concluding they do not have much in common.

Any lifestyle depends to a degree on determining how exclusive it will be. A young person who is very involved in tennis will spend a good deal of her time doing that activity or at least planning around it, talking about it, and so forth. A peer who has little interest in tennis is likely to drift off to others who have similar interests to her. This is no different to using drugs. If someone enjoys tennis but it is not a major theme in her life, then she will tend to have a wider variety of peers than those who are heavily involved in tennis. If she uses drugs not very regularly she can also have using and non-using peers. Most people end up being recreational drug or alcohol users and thus can maintain a peer group that has both using and non-using peers.

The teenage years are when this jockeying and negotiating with peer groups occurs in earnest. It continues throughout life, but in the teenage years it is particularly prominent as they discover what they like and what they want out of life. They try different things, including drugs and tennis, some of which they will like and others they will not, and in varying degrees. This will determine the peer group they end up with. Drugs do not "grab" teenagers and drag them in, as is sometimes portrayed in the popular press. Yes, there are times where a teenager will be influenced by peers to take drugs when they would prefer not to. If the teenager is opposed to it, this rarely lasts for any significant length of time and they will leave the peer group. Any addiction they may develop will not keep them there for any great period of time. It's much more about the lifestyle and what one wants out of life. If they do not like using drugs but the lifestyle is OK they can be influenced for some time, but they are not being strongly coerced into doing something they do not want to do. If the peer group of the ambivalent teenage drug user changes he can quite easily stop using for long periods of time as the drug has no other psychological importance to him, unlike for the dependent and symptomatic user. In the long run the dependent drug user will end up with a peer group of other dependent drug users. If a teenager does not have the psyche of a dependent drug user, then sooner or later he will leave that peer group. It's just not how he goes about living life.

Working with the teenage client

When conducting a workshop in Serbia titled "Working with Teenagers," one of the participants, Ljiljana Jerinic (pers. comm. 2009), asked a question that left me perplexed. I was asked about my approach to the counseling of teenagers and did I come from a parental position? That is, do I see myself in a parent-type role to the teenager? This did not necessarily mean in a Critical Parent-type of role, but overall did I feel like a parent-type person when working with a teenager.

My initial response to the question was, "Yes and no," which is obviously an ambiguous response and an unsatisfactory one. In subsequent discussion I was asked if I did not see myself in a clear parent position, did I relate to the teenager in more of a of peer role? Like a friend to the teenager. The answer to this was a more definite "No." However, if I did not come from a parent-type role or a friend-type role, what was my role? The answer eventually turned out to involve a comprehensive and complex array of relationships which I had evolved over the years of working with teenagers. I had intuitively arrived at this therapeutic approach without being consciously aware of what I had been doing.

To begin articulating the answer to the question, this section will describe the overall structure of the therapeutic relationship when working with the teenage drug user. Figure 10.3 illustrates the therapeutic situation I am wanting to set up with the various parties. This is the best case scenario and will occur in varying degrees depending on the cooperation of the parties involved.

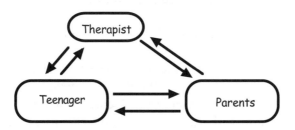

Figure 10.3 Structure of the therapeutic relationship when working with teenagers

In counseling the teenager I want the parents or those who are responsible for the teenager to be involved. The parents have vastly more direct contact with the teenager than I and therefore the more they relate to the teenager in a way that will support the therapeutic goals the better. Most often they are willing to be involved (at least one of them) but at times they refuse, or they may simply not be around all that much. The teenager will agree to be involved in varying degrees. Some are quite willing, others are clearly unwilling but attend because they are either court ordered or the parents have made them by using some kind of coercion. At times the teenager may be quite unwilling initially but over time his attitude changes and he begins to cooperate as he sees some benefit coming from it.

I do not restrict myself in any way with who I will counsel and in what configuration. I will engage directly both the parents and the teenager, as Figure 10.3 shows, and will involve myself directly in the relationship between the teenager and parents. I will see them in any combination that becomes necessary as the therapy process proceeds. I will see the teenager individually, mother and father individually, the parents as a couple, the teenager with one parent (mother or father), and all three of them together. At times others may be involved, such as siblings or other close family or friends. Sometimes I will do a lot of counseling with the parents and at other times very little. Who I see is determined by what is currently happening with the teenager, their drug use, and the other parties involved.

Most often the age of the teenager is directly inverse to the importance of the parents in the process. If the teenager is 14 years old the parents are usually central in the therapy process. If the teenager is 19, then they are usually less involved. However, if there is an enmeshed family structure, then the parents remain pivotal to the process until the teenager can gain some kind of psychological separation.

Figure 10.3 is to scale in terms of the relationships of the four parties. I want to establish myself off to the side of the relationship between parents and teenager but a bit closer to the teenager. I am working primarily with the teenager, not the parents, as the teenager is the one who is defined as the problem with some kind of drug use. This rationale allows for more "connection" between myself and the teenager. To assist with this I always ask the parents if it's OK for me not to repeat to them what the teenager has said to me (excluding highly dangerous behavior). Invariably they say "Yes," which I then communicate to the teenager. I want to create kind of a special relationship between the teenager and myself.

I want to establish myself in the teenager's mind as a trusted confidant and advisor who is not working for the parents or the courts. I am not with the parents and at the same time I am not against the parents. This is at times a hard position to maintain. I try to sit off to the side of the teenager–parent relationship in this way. I do not side with the teenager against the parents and I do not take the parents' side against the teenager. At times the teenage client may try and force me to take one of those positions and I must avoid doing so. I endeavor to maintain a type of neutrality with the parents and teenager. At times this is easy to do and at other times one party may take the position, "If you are not with me, then you are against me." This needs to be avoided if at all possible.

The more emotionally important I become for the teenager the better. I want to be benign, in the sense of not being seen as an adversary but if he can emotionally depend on me this is a desirable situation, especially if I can take the role of confidant and advisor.

I actively intervene in the relationship between the parents and the teenager. Indeed I can use this to keep my position off to the side. For instance, at times parents need to put limits and controls on the teenager. I will discuss with them how they do this and encourage it. This in one way is not fair to the parents, as they take all the heat and it allows me to avoid conflict with the teenager and remain in the position I am in Figure 10.3. If the parents are seen as the adversaries, then I am less likely to be seen as an adversary and a benign type of relationship can be fostered. As I said above, the parents have vastly more contact with the teenager than I do. It is clearly advantageous to create a relationship between the teenager and the parents that will support the therapeutic endeavour to stop or modify the teenager's drug use.

Working with the teenage drug user is not simply a matter of taking a parental role or position with them. My original answer of "Yes and no" is now explicable, because I do take a type of parental position with them but it is a very specific parental position. It is not the usual parental role like that of a mother or father. Instead it is the specific position of being a benign advisor and confidant in a complex set of relationships, often involving four or more people.

Further aspects of relating to the teenage drug user

Figure 10.4 is how I would rate myself on the continuum from highly authoritarian to highly permissive. This is how I behave and transact as a counselor with a drug-using client. Indeed, this would be true for all age groups, but is especially true when relating to the teenage drug or alcohol user. Of course it varies with different types of clients, and with the same client over time, but overall this sums up the approach I take.

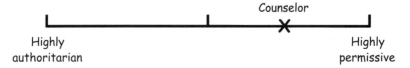

Figure 10.4 Position the counselor takes with the teenage drug user

Clearly I view myself at the permissive end of the spectrum. At a recent supervision group I made a statement that was met with surprise and disquiet by the some of the supervisees. I stated that I would never tell a drug-using client not to use. Again that applies for all age groups but is especially so for the teenage user. In transactional analysis terms I rarely use the Critical Parent or Controlling Parent ego state when working with teenagers. This makes for a permissive type of counselor in this way at least. This, however, creates a dilemma.

The reason why I would not tell a teenage drug user not to use or make statements that drug use is bad is because you quickly lose the client. He will quickly slip into the Child ego state and either stop coming, attend sessions but not tell me what he has been using, or take more drugs because he has moved into a rebellious position against me. If you want the teenager to remain open, frank, and see you as an advisor/confidant, then you cannot say such things to them.

On the other hand, by not saying such things, I am tacitly giving him permission to use drugs and thus supporting his drug use in that way. Through transference the client will introject me to varying degrees into their Parent ego state. If I am not saying, "Don't do drugs," then he is not introjecting that, such that their Parental record of me is in one way supporting his drug use. It seems we have the good and the bad in this dilemma. Obviously I see it as more important not to "lose" the client, as I said before, versus providing a Parent model that is clearly against drug use being introjected into his Parent ego state.

A common transaction found with teenage drug users is shown in Figure 10.5.

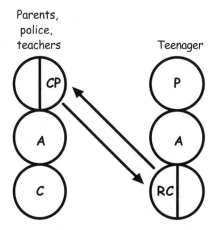

Figure 10.5 Critical Parent to Rebellious Child Transaction

The parents and teenager can become locked into this type of transaction. This can, and does, go on for long periods of time and gets nowhere; indeed it usually just alienates the two parties. Any discussion between them often ends up like this, so relating from other ego states diminishes and they get caught into this single way of relating. Not uncommonly when a teenager is brought to counseling this type of transaction is prominent in the family life.

Also not uncommonly, the teenager who enters counseling is also expecting me to respond to him from the finger-wagging Critical Parent ego state. This needs to be avoided. If I do this, or am even perceived to do this, then the counseling process is severely compromised. If the counselor and teenage drug user establish a Critical Parent to Rebellious Child set of transactions, then the therapeutic gain for the teenager will be minimal.

Why are the gains so minimal? With this transactional dynamic one essentially has a conflict-based relationship where the battle lines are drawn. When the two parties are in battle the goals stop being about the relationship or therapeutic gain. Both sides have little interest in understanding or empathizing with the other, instead the goal becomes about winning or who becomes the dominant party in the relationship. Even if one party should win and the other complies, what is the "loser" going to do psychologically? They are not going to like losing, will resent the "winner," and bide their time until circumstances allow them to come out fighting again. If the counselor is using his or her Critical Parent ego state a significant amount, he or she needs to consider what the underlying agenda is in counseling the teenager.

In drug counseling this is particularly important. As it is often about illegal drug use or the inappropriate consumption of alcohol, people feel more free to express Critical Parent and judgmental views to the client. They feel they have the backing of society at large and thus are doing a good thing for society as they "tell off" the teenage user. Even if the teenager does stop, he is doing so because of an outside Critical Parent and not from any internal motivation. With drug use, when there is little internal motivation to stop, there unlikely to be a lasting period of abstinence.

So often when the teenager enters therapy he has already put me in the authority or Critical Parent ego state position. There is little I can do about this and thus I have to duck and weave when he shoots his Rebellious Child transactions at me, so that I do not respond from the Critical Parent. Sometimes the teenager will even perceive me to be responding from the Critical Parent when I am not. At least in the early stages of counseling I work at avoiding the Critical Parent to Rebellious Child dynamic developing between myself and the teenager. If it does develop, as I said before, there will be little growth or long-term psychological gain for the teenager.

How does one avoid the Critical Parent response to the Rebellious Child transaction? To any transaction the counselor has six possible responses, these being:

- Critical Parent
- Nurturing Parent
- Adult
- Conforming Child
- Rebellious Child
- Free Child.

The counselor can respond from any of these ego states. Only one of them, the Critical Parent ego state, will encourage further rebelliousness. All the other responses will encourage the teenager to switch ego states and respond from a non-rebellious ego state. The three most obvious ways of responding are with the Adult, Free Child, and Nurturing Parent ego states.

For example, the teenager may make a rebellious transaction with the comment, "I have scored some good ecstasy for the weekend."

The counselor can respond from any of the six ego states but the most productive will be the three just mentioned. For example:

Adult: "Is it a dance party you are going to?"

"Where do you go after you leave here?"

Nurturing Parent: "I worry about you, so will you make sure you're safe?"

"Can I look at that cut on your hand to see if it's OK?"

Free Child: "Did you hear the one about the dyslexic guy who walked into a bar?"

"That's a cool shirt you have on today."

Each of these responses crosses the teenager's initial transaction and responds in a way he did not anticipate. Each puts pressure on him to move out of his rebellious frame of mind. The most common one, and easiest to do, is the Adult ego state response. Just ask a question. This crosses the transaction, as shown in Figure 10.6.

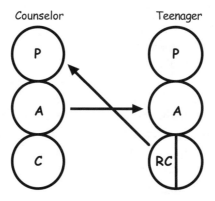

Figure 10.6 Crossing the transaction with the Adult ego state

The teenager starts with a Rebellious transaction. Instead of responding with the Critical Parent the counselor responds with the Adult ego state, as shown. The easiest way to do this is to ask a simple question.

Teenager in RC: "I have scored some good ecstasy for the weekend."

Counselor in Adult: "Where is the dance party?"

As can be seen this crosses the transaction. Not only does it avoid a battle forming between the teenager and the counselor, it also pressures the teenager to move out of his Rebellious Child and into his Adult ego state. As Figure 10.6 shows, the counselor is stimulating the Adult ego state in the teenager, making it more likely to be used in the next response to the counselor. If this happens the counselor has avoided creating a Rebellious Child–Critical Parent dynamic forming between them.

The Nurturing Parent ego state response pressures the teenager to move into the Free Child ego state and feel nurtured rather than attacked by the Critical Parent. The same will happen if the counselor responds from his own Free Child. This encourages a Free Child response from the teenager rather than a Rebellious Child response. This is an especially productive transaction for counselors to do in any form of counseling. If a good deal of Free Child to Free Child transactions occur between the counselor and client that creates a most productive therapeutic environment. However, one needs to be more careful than with the Adult response as a Free Child response can sometimes be taken as a glib or frivolous response, which may result in the client feeling put down.

In the early stages of counseling the teenager, there may be many times he uses such rebellious transactions, looking for a Critical Parent response. If such critical responses can be avoided, after a time he will use them less, and a solid basis for the therapeutic relationship has been established. The foundations for being seen as a benign confidant and advisor are being well laid.

Teenage drug use and family structure

If the teenager comes from an enmeshed family structure there may be other factors to consider when counseling. In the enmeshed family, people are too close and too involved. There is a sense of a very clear boundary between inside the family and outside the family. Members have a sense of closeness and belonging but overly so. In the enmeshed family there can be a sense of not trusting others outside the family, so the only people you can really trust are family members. There can even be some paranoid beliefs about non-family members and an "us and them" type of thinking. There may be disputes that arise with others outside the family and this creates a sense of unity amongst family members. Family gatherings like birthdays and Christmas are very important and non-attendance is usually viewed in a very dim light.

The parents may have few external friends and will use family members for their social relationships. They may go to few non-family parties, have few non-family parties at home, and rarely invite others to the house to socialize. The opposite to this family structure is the distancing family. In this instance there are tenuous connections between family members and often there is no contact for long periods of time. There is little sense of belonging and little sense of the family being a close-knit group with a clear sense of boundary between it and the rest of the world. The lack of sense of belonging or community leaves family members feeling isolated. There may be one person who holds the family together, and when they die or move away the family disintegrates. There is little interest in or frequency of family gatherings. They can easily geographically move away from each other and there are long periods of little or no communication, with few protests from other family members.

A teenager who grows up in the enmeshed type of family structure has a special difficulty. Jay Haley, in his landmark book *Leaving Home* (1980), describes the teenage stage of development as the "leaving home" stage of development. The teenager has reached a level of maturity in his psychological development such that he is ready to leave home, both physically and psychologically. Sometimes this stage is referred to as the stage of psychological birth, where a new, psychologically complete, human being is born. The parents are no longer required to fulfill the psychological functions they once did for the teenager and so he can leave them.

However, parents can make leaving home quite difficult if they so choose and the teenager may find the concept of leaving quite frightening himself. These psychological forces can combine in various ways such that the parents and teenager unconsciously set up a situation that stops the teenager leaving. One way to do this is to get sick. Such sickness can include depression, anxiety (particularly agoraphobia), anorexia, suicidal feelings, or a drug problem. If the teenager remains sick, then he cannot leave home, or at least it keeps the parents involved in a significant way in the teenager's life. If a drug problem develops at this stage of development, one needs to look for this type of dynamic going on, or this type of causation for the problematic drug use. I have found it at times to be a strong factor and at other times nonexistent.

If it does play a role, then the therapy is about facilitating the psychological separation of the teenager from the parents, so that he can reach a psychological birth. How successful and easy this is also depends on the attitude of the parents. If all parties are prepared to address what needs to be addressed, then the drug issues can subside quite substantially in a relatively short space of time. However, this is not always the case. At times the teenager can be a good distraction for both parents. If they can focus on the problem the teenager has, that allows them to be distracted from other problems which may exist, such as marital problems. If the teenager leaves home the parents may be forced to start looking at their own marriage because there is now no distraction and that may result in marital breakdown. The point being made here is that at times there can be strong psychological forces independent of the teenager that are pressuring him to maintain a drug problem.

Hot potato

Finally we have the concept of the hot potato. In this case the teenager and a parent establish a relationship where the teenager takes on the psychological difficulties of the parent (they take the hot potato from the parent). This allows the parent to avoid her own difficulties as they are projected onto the teenager and she can then deal with them in the teenager. If she has her own self-destructive urges, these can be projected onto the teenager, who starts to take them on by developing a drug problem. Thus two advantages are obtained, first she can avoid her own difficulties and second she can give to her biological child what her own Child ego state wants. By meeting the needs of her son with such things as care and comforting she can gain vicarious satisfaction for her own Child ego state, which wants the same.

This is not as uncommon as one may think. Indeed in professions such as counseling it can and does happen. By becoming a counselor one can achieve the same. If one goes to work each day and is confronted by needy people in pain this can allow the counselor to be distracted from their own Child ego state pain. In addition it is not uncommonly acknowledged that some counselors end up with clients who tend to have histories and issues that are similar to the counselor's. People who have suffered child abuse end up counseling clients who have suffered similar abuse. Counselors who have had drug problems end up becoming drug counselors. Indeed there are some drug-counseling agencies that will only employ counselors who have had a drug use history of their own. It is quite possible the counselor is gaining some kind of vicarious satisfaction by giving the client the care that their own Child ego state wants.

This is by no means necessarily a negative. Indeed it is inevitable, as that is how many humans function. People tend to become involved in pursuits that have some personal significance for them. I would suggest the majority of people do this at least to some degree. In giving care of some kind to a client, the counselor can also vicariously benefit. There is nothing wrong with this, as long as the client benefits from it, which happens in the majority of cases.

It seems safe to say the mother–child attachment is the strongest attachment any person experiences in their life. It is the most important attachment of all, and in it, all kinds of unconscious negotiation goes on from day one. From birth, mother and child learn how to dance together. They work together to form a partnership that works for both of them (White 1990a). Many, many subtle and not so subtle communication patterns and behavior patterns are negotiated and established (Klaus and Klaus 1985), the majority being out of awareness of both mother and child. Most result in healthy communication patterns, but sometimes they result in self-defeating communication styles and the hot potato can be one of those. The child unconsciously learns that to display the angst of mother or father gets subtle approval and it forms one of the basic structures of the relationship. He learns that this is how life is and that is one of his roles in life.

In this case, as with the leaving home problem, the counselor needs to understand the relationship dynamics in the client's life in order to understand why the drug use is occurring. When diagnosed, the counselor deals with the problem drug behavior in the usual way, such as with motivational interviewing, establishing triggers, and so forth. In addition the counselor also needs to address the problem relationships in the client's life, assisting the teenager to finally leave home or, how to drop the hot potato that has been passed on to him.

Parents and the teenager

In counseling teenage drug users one commonly has to also counsel the parents or some person who is deemed to be the guardian of the teenager. The remainder of this chapter is devoted to this topic and covers issues that the drug counselor is often confronted with by parents.

The bottom line, or the most important thing for parents to keep in mind, is to keep the lines of communication open. It is most important to maintain some kind of relationship and communication with the teenager, to allow the teenager to have some sense of belonging to a family or feeling like they have some kind of relationship with some family-like person. People who have a sense of belonging in a relationship or a family are much more psychologically robust and resilient than those who do not.

The worst scenario is to have a teenager who feels alone and alienated. He is vulnerable to exploitation by others and is more likely to engage in dangerous behaviors, including dangerous drug taking and drinking. If parents want their teenager to be more resilient to peer pressure the best way to do that is to maintain a good quality relationship with him. The less communication the teenager has with the parents the more influential the peer group becomes.

At times the teenager will do things which parents find most unattractive, immoral, and "wrong." In such circumstances it is very easy for parents to get angry and push the teenager away. Parents in essence have to "sideline" their own value system and feelings, at least to some extent, and at least temporarily, in order to maintain a relationship of some quality. Obviously that is a difficult thing for many parents to do. Fortunately adolescence is a phase which most move through, so it is temporary. As a rule of thumb, when a teenager becomes an adult he will adopt about 70 to 80 percent of the same values in his Parent ego state as the parents have in theirs. Many adults can think back to things they did as a teenager which they would never do now because they have a different value system and beliefs about life and the world. In the final analysis, the point being made here is for the parent to do as much as possible to keep the lines of communication open with the teenager and maintain a sense of relationship between the two of them.

Do not panic

When parents suspect or have proof their teenager is taking drugs most will understandably feel anxiety, at times considerable anxiety. It is easy to catastrophize and conjure up images of their child ending up a prostitute or lying in some tenement, semi-conscious, with a needle hanging out of their arm.

The counselor first needs to set about reducing the anxiety of the parents and provide them with information. This can be done relatively easily with information on statistics and a discussion about the different types of drug use. The majority of drinkers and drug users are recreational users, and the drug will cause little to no negative consequences in their lives. There is a much smaller group who do go on to symptomatic and dependent drug use, so that is a possibility but unlikely.

In the section titled, "Why teenagers use drugs," earlier in this chapter, the signs one can look for were explained. The signs which show that the teenager may be developing a pattern of dependent use were also explained. The counselor would provide this type of information to the parents to be alert for. However, the teenager may not wish to be that candid with the parents in answering such questions about his drug use and this is where a counselor may be useful. The majority of parents do not have much to worry about as the drug use will never develop into a harmful pattern.

Scare tactics

Due to the anxiety of discovering their teenager uses drugs many parents immediately jump into using scare tactics. They think, "I will tell my son drugs are very dangerous, then he will be scared and not use them." An understandable reaction but one to avoid, if possible. The problem of scare tactics is stated consistently in the literature. Indeed a pamphlet produced by the Western Australian Police Service (1996) states, "Try to avoid using scare tactics to frighten the child away from drug use. You may lose credibility in their eyes especially if they know from their own or others' experiences that what you are saying is not true or exaggerated" (p.2). An insightful statement indeed by the police.

Besides the problem of the teenager realizing the parents are using scare tactics and the resultant loss of credibility, scare tactics do not work, especially on the young drug user. Teenagers as a group tend to be egocentric, narcissistic, and feel they are special and omnipotent. They feel the general rules do not apply to them because of their "specialness." From a personality point of view teenagers are different to the general adult population.

As a result, if told drugs are dangerous, they will have a sense that somehow they are the exception to the rule and they will not be hurt or killed by drugs. As discussed earlier, they are poor risk assessors and thus see drugs as not being a high risk to them, and hence the scare factor is reduced in the scare tactics approach.

However, there is even more to the concepts of scare tactics and risk. The criminal personality, with which the teenager has some similarities, commonly has a lack of anxiety (Midgley 1993). They do not feel anxious or at least are not aware of being anxious or scared. In particular, they do not find what are normally scary activities particularly anxiety producing. This allows them to more easily cross the line and engage in illegal acts such as bank robberies and so forth. If there is little anxiety, then a scary activity is no longer scary.

To smuggle drugs though a country which has the death penalty for trafficking, the average adult would find extremely scary. The average adult could not strap drugs to their torso and walk through customs at an airport. Most would find that so anxiety producing they would either faint or become incapacitated in some way, so that they would immediately grab much unwanted attention. The criminal personality and youth are more capable of doing such a thing as they do not feel anxiety in the same way that the average adult does.

If a teenager is told that injecting drugs is dangerous, they will understand what is being said and why it is dangerous. However, their Child ego state will not find it scary as they feel less anxiety when confronted with a scary event. Thus this is another reason why scare tactics with the young tends to not work. Parents and counselors need to stop assuming that the teenager experiences the world the same way they do. Before concluding, there is one other area of scare tactics that needs to be discussed.

Unfortunately there is no polite way to put it. Scare tactics involves not telling the truth and scare tactics involves being dishonest. In scare tactics certain information is withheld and other information is exaggerated. If parents exaggerate the dangers, then, as the quote from the Police Service above shows, they will loose the credibility and respect of the teenager. In Chapter 2, I quoted a 16-year-old English boy who discovered that smoking marijuana rarely resulted in the smoker ending up a glassy-eyed junkie wasting away in a den full of drug addicts. Instead, he observed that for most people there were very few negative effects from smoking marijuana.

This 16-year-old realized that he had not been told the full truth by those whom he trusted, who had given him misinformation about smoking marijuana. This can damage the relationship between teenager and parent at a time when one wants it to be strong.

Dealing with a disclosure by a teenager

If a teenager discloses he is using do you tell him to stop or not? Some parents have clear moral views on drugs and no drug use is permitted at all. Other parents simply believe it is necessary to make very clear that drug use is not permissible. These statements give the teenager a very clear boundary about what is and what is not acceptable behavior. Any developmental psychology text would say this is a healthy thing to do in child rearing. With drugs, however, it is more complex.

The danger in doing this is that the teenager withdraws further from the relationship with his parents. He continues to take drugs and simply does not tell them. He feels he can no longer talk to them about drugs, thus increasing his sense of isolation, and the parents lose further influence over the teenager in this way. Psychology texts on child development would say this is an unhealthy thing. The parents are stuck between a rock and a hard place. There is a negative attached to either decision made. It seems the two choices are:

1. Being clear and telling a teenager that drug use is not OK. This sets a clear boundary for the teenager, thus reducing the possibility of drug use. However, this increases the possibility of damage to the relationship between parent and teenager where the teenager withdraws, causing an increased sense of isolation, which increases the possibility of prolonged drug use.

2. Encouraging the teenager to be open and talk about his drug use. This does not set a clear boundary for the teenager, thus increasing the possibility of drug use. This encourages the teenager to be open and frank in his relationship with the

parent, thus allowing for a feeling of connection and support, which decreases the possibility of prolonged drug use.

Some may argue that you can do both. You can tell him not to take drugs and still be able to listen to him about his drug use. I disagree. The very act of listening to the teenager talk about his drug use and discussing it with him automatically implies at least tacit agreement with the act of taking drugs. Also, as soon as you state that no drug use is OK, it is likely you are going to get at the very least a modified version of what is really happening with his drug taking. Unfortunately, in my view it is not possible to have it both ways.

A difficult situation indeed, and perhaps the answer depends on the personality of the teenager. If he tends to be compliant, choice 1 may be more effective. If he is rebellious and strong willed, choice 2 may be the better way to go. Alternatively one can split the choices between people. In the previous chapter I discussed my role or position in counseling teenagers. It could be suggested that the parents can take choice 1 with the teenager and I take choice 2, thus allowing for the benefits of both if correctly managed. It seems safe to say that the solution here must be assessed on an individual basis, depending on the views of the parents and the personality of the teenager and others who can play various roles with him.

Urine testing teenagers

Sometimes parents consider the option of drug testing their teenage son or daughter. Urine-testing kits are relatively cheap and can be easily obtained from many pharmacies. However, I recommend parents do not do this for a variety of reasons.

What do you do if a positive result is obtained? By the time it gets to the point where parents consider drug-testing the teenager, all other forms of punishment and loss of privileges have usually been exhausted with little success. Some parents may say, "Well, at least we will know for sure she is taking drugs." Certainty is indeed a positive thing but it still does not answer the question, "What do you do now?" If the teenager gives a positive result and there are no repercussions, then nothing is really achieved by doing the drug test in the first place. Do you eject her from the home or continue with punishments that have minimal effect? Throwing a teenager out is a very serious thing to do and will almost certainly result in increased drug use.

When it gets to the point of considering such drug tests it's a sign the relationship has reached the point of significant disarray. The parent–teenager relationship is in a state of disrepair and in my view such drug testing is only going to make it worse. It simply provides one more thing for the teenager and her parents to argue about. Allegations of not being trusted are made by the teenager and allegations of not being trustworthy are made by the parents, often with shouting and swearing included.

Without a doubt the most powerful influence to prevent a teenager from taking drugs, especially taking drugs dangerously, is a good relationship with the parents. As stated earlier in this chapter, if the teenager has a sense of good connection with an adult in their life, he is more psychologically robust and hence less likely to engage in some kind of self-destructive behavior. My suggestion is to forget the drug testing and work at getting the relationship back on track.

Some teenagers can take it as a challenge and will endeavour to outwit the tester, which only further damages the relationship. Furthermore, urine is easy to obtain, store, and hide. It is no use doing a urine test for drugs unless you know the sample given is current and from the person being tested. To make sure of this one needs to watch the person urinating. To do this parents require the teenager to expose their genitals for the them to look at. This, as you can imagine, will also damage the relationship.

Conclusion

Psychologically teenagers are quite different to the mature adult. As a result they require special consideration when being examined psychologically and when looking at how to assist them therapeutically. Due to the teenager's psychological immaturity she cannot be considered in isolation and thus the counselor must consider the immediate family as well. With adults this is less of a necessity.

This chapter attempted to show some of the pitfalls and possible solutions for parents when dealing with a teenager who is using drugs. It is indeed a difficult thing to do as there are many delicate situations, but if handled correctly they can be dealt with without too much trouble. On the other hand, if things do not go well serious difficulties can arise. The idea of teenagers using drugs is an anxiety-producing one. Their youthful exuberance can get them into trouble in so many ways, none more so than in using drugs and alcohol.

This chapter also discussed in some detail how the counselor can establish a working therapeutic relationship with the teenager and the parents. This involves endeavoring to establish a set of relationships amongst the various family members and the counselor that are more likely lead to a positive outcome. Owing to the maturity level of the teenager it is deemed necessary to include the parents to some degree, unlike with the fully mature adult drug user.

Chapter 11

Epilogue

The study of this book—counseling alcohol and drug users—is now complete. Finally it is important to highlight that drug counseling has some unique features compared to other areas of counseling. The drug counselor, compared to the generalist counselor, has a more difficult task to master. Most problem drug users are ambivalent about their drug use—they want to stop and they want to continue. On the other hand, the client who goes to general counseling for depression does not have depression ambivalence, the client who has insomnia does not have insomnia ambivalence. As a result these clients are naturally more motivated to change than a drug-using client and in the counseling profession client motivation is probably one of the most important things of all. The drug counselor has a more onerous task in this way.

However, that is not all. Drugs are an emotive issue and people can have quite strong feelings about the topic of drugs and drug use. In addition, drugs are for many a moral issue as well. This complicates matters for the drug counselor in a way that does not affect the generalist counselor. Some drug counselors decide not to do harm minimization with clients.

Did they come to this conclusion because they believe that it promotes drug use?

Did they come to this conclusion because they see it as morally wrong to teach a drug user how to use drugs?

If they do have a moral issue with it do they have the right to impose that view onto the client by not engaging in harm minimization?

These are significant questions that have no clear answer. Each and every drug counselor must ask and answer these questions for themselves. This clouds the field of drug counseling in a way that is not so for generalist counselor. If a client presents for counseling with panic attacks the situation is clear. There is no moral question about a person having panic attacks and the area of panic does not engender strong feelings as the issue of drugs can. People do not generally have a moral issue about the person who suffers from insomnia, so the treatment of such a person is not clouded by the esoteric questions that the drug counselor must answer before he can begin. In conclusion, this needs to be recognized, acknowledged, and drug counselors need to be commended for taking on the difficult task that they do. They are certainly needed in almost every society; it is a problem that is not going to go away soon.

References

American Psychiatric Association (1994) *Diagnostic and Statistical Manual of Mental Disorders,* (4th edn). Washington, DC: American Psychiatric Association.

American Psychiatric Association (2000) *Diagnostic and Statistical Manual of Mental Disorders,* (4th edn–text revision). Washington, DC: American Psychiatric Association.

Anglin, D., Hser, Y., and Grella, C. (1997) "Drug addiction and treatment careers among clients in DATOS." *Psychology of Addictive Behavior 11,* 308–323.

Australian Institute of Health and Welfare (2007) *2007 National Drug Strategy Household Survey.* Canberra: Australian Institute of Health and Welfare.

Australian Psychological Society (2005) *Perspectives in Psychology: Substance Use.* Melbourne: Australian Psychological Society.

Australian Psychological Society (2011) *Guidelines for the Use of Therapeutic Aversive Procedures.* Melbourne: Australian Psychological Society.

Beck, A. (1967) *Depression: Experimental and Theoretical Aspects.* London: Staples Press.

Berne, E. (1957) *A Layman's Guide to Psychiatry and Psychoanalysis.* New York: Simon and Schuster.

Berne, E. (1964) *Games People Play.* New York: Grove Press.

Berne, E. (1972) *What Do You Say After You Say Hello?.* New York: Grove Press.

Best, D., Day, E., Cantillano, V., Gaston, R.L. *et al.* (2008) "Mapping heroin careers: Utilising a standardised history-taking method to assess the speed of escalation of heroin using careers in a treatment-seeking cohort." *Drug and Alcohol Review 27,* 165–170.

Best, D.W., Ghufran, S., Day, E., Ray, R. *et al.* (2008) "Breaking the habit: A retrospective analysis of desistance factors among formerly problematic heroin users." *Drug and Alcohol Review 27,* 619–624.

Bowlby, J. (1971) *Attachment.* Harmondsworth: Pelican.

Brennan, K.A. and Shaver, P.R. (1995) "Dimensions of adult attachment, affect regulation, and romantic relationship functioning." *Personality and Social Psychology Bulletin 21,* 267–283.

Carr, S. and Francis, A. (2009) "Childhood maltreatment and adult personality disorder symptoms in a non-clinical sample." *Australian Psychologist 44,* 3, 146–155.

Collins, J.K. (1991) "Research into adolescence: A forgotten era." *Australian Psychologist 26,* 1, 1–9.

Cooper, M.L., Shaver, P.R., and Collins, N.L. (1998) "Attachment styles, emotion regulation, and adjustment in adolescence." *Journal of Personality and Social Psychology 74,* 1380–1397.

Craighead, W.E. and Nemeroff, C.B. (2004) *The Concise Corsini Encyclopedia of Psychology and Behavioral Science.* New Jersey: John Wiley & Sons.

Crawford, J., Rodden, P., Kippax, S., and Van de Ven, P. (1998) "Negotiated safety and agreements between men in relationships: Are all agreements equal?" *International Conference on AIDS 12*, 362 (abstract no. 25/23105).

Darke, S., Mills, K.L., Ross, J., Williamson, A. *et al.* (2009) "The ageing heroin user: Career length, clinical profile and outcomes across 36 months." *Drug and Alcohol Review 28*, 243–249.

De Rick, A., Vanheule, S., and Vanhaeghe, P. (2009) "Alcohol addiction and the attachment system: An empirical study of attachment style, alexithymia, and psychiatric disorders in alcoholic inpatients." *Substance Use and Misuse 44*, 99–114.

Dear, L. (1995) "Negotiated safety: What you don't know won't hurt you, or will it?" *Drug and Alcohol Review 14*, 3, 323–329.

Gatz, M., Mortimer, J., Fratiglioni, L. *et al.* (2007) "Accounting for the relationship between low education and dementia. a twin study." *Physiological Behavior 92*, 232–237.

Giroud, C., Augsburger, M., Sadeghipour, F., Varesio, E. *et al.* (1997) "Ecstasy—the status in French-speaking Switzerland. Composition of seized drugs, analysis of biological specimens and short review of its pharmacological action and toxicity." *Schweiz Rundsch Med Prax 86*, 510–523.

Goulding, M.M. and Goulding, R.L. (1979) *Changing Lives through Redecision Therapy.* New York: Brunner/Mazel Publishers.

Government of Western Australia—Drug and Alcohol Office (2008) *Cannabis: The Facts. Drug Aware.* Available at www.dao.health.wa.gov.au/DesktopModules/Bring2mind/DMX/Download.aspx?Command=Core_Download&EntryId=339&PortalId=0&TabId=211, accessed May 2, 2012.

Graham, J.R. (1990) *MMPI-2: Assessing Personality and Psychopathology.* New York: Oxford University Press.

Greene, R.L. (1980) *The MMPI: An Interpretive Manual.* New York: Grune & Stratton.

Gross, M. (2010) "Alcoholics anonymous: Still sober after 75 years." *American Journal of Public Health 100*, 12, 2361–2363.

Guzman, R., Colfax, G.N., Wheeler, S., Mansergh, G. *et al.* (2005) "Negotiated safety relationships and sexual behaviour among a diverse sample of HIV-negative men who have sex with men." *JAIDS 38*, 1, 82–86.

Haley, J. (1980) *Leaving Home: The Therapy of Disturbed Young People.* London: McGraw-Hill.

Helfgott, S. (1997) *Module 9 Assessment. Participant's Handbook. Volunteer Drug and Alcohol Counsellor's Training Program.* Perth: Government of Western Australia Drug and Alcohol Office.

Helfgott, S. and Allsop, S. (1997) *Module 7 Models of Addiction. Participant's Handbook. Volunteer Drug and Alcohol Counsellor's Training Program.* Perth: Government of Western Australia Drug and Alcohol Office.

Hickman, M., Carrivick, S., Paterson, S., Hunt, N. *et al.* (2006) "London audit of drug-related overdose deaths: Characteristics and typology, and implications for prevention and monitoring." *Addiction 102*, 317–323.

Kandel, D.B. and Faust, R. (1975) "Sequences and stages in patterns of adolescent drug use." *Archives of General Psychiatry 32*, 923–932.

Kelly, J.F., Magill, M., and Stout, R.L. (2009) "How do people recover from alcohol dependence? A systematic review of the research on mechanisms of behavior change in Alcoholics Anonymous." *Addiction Research and Theory 17*, 3, 236–259.

Kerr, D., Dietze, P., Kelly, A., and Jolley, D. (2009) "Improved response by peers after witnessed heroin overdose in Melbourne." *Drug and Alcohol Review 28*, 327–330.

Kippax, S., Crawford, J., Davis, M., Rodden, P. *et al.* (1993) "Sustaining safe sex: A longitudinal study of homosexual men." *AIDS 7*, 257–263.

Kippax, S., Crawford, J., Noble, J., Prestage, G. *et al.* (1997) "Sexual negotiation in the AIDS era: Negotiated safety revisited." *AIDS 11*, 191–197.

Kissen, M. (2006) "Increasing executive and 'self-soothing' capacities in the treatment of addictive disorders." *Bulletin of the Menninger Clinic 70*, 3, 202–209.

Klaus, M.H. and Klaus, P.H. (1985) *The Amazing Newborn*. Sydney: Addison-Wesley.

Krystal, H. (1978) "Self-representation and the capacity for self-care." *Annual of Psychoanalysis 6*, 209–247.

Laffaye, C., McKellar, J.D., Ilgen, M.A., and Moos, R.H. (2008) "Predictors of 4-year outcome of community residential treatment for patients with substance use disorders." *Addiction 103*, 671–680.

Lende, D.H., Leonard, T., Sterk, C.E., and Elifson, K. (2007) "Functional methamphetamine use: An insider's perspective." *Addiction Research and Theory 15*, 5, 465–477.

Lustig, C. and Buckner, R. (2004) "Preserved neural correlates of priming in old age and dementia." *Neuron 42*, 865–875.

Lynskey, M.T., Vink, J.M., and Boomsma, D.I. (2006) "Early onset cannabis use and progression to other drug use in a sample of Dutch twins." *Behavior Genetics 36*, 2, 195–200.

Mahler, M. (1965) "On the significance of the normal separation–individuation phase." In M. Schur (ed.) *Drives, Affects and Behaviour*. New York: International Universities Press.

Mahler, M., Pine, F., and Bergman, A. (1975) *The Psychological Birth of the Human Infant*. New York: Praeger.

Marsh, A. and Dale, A. (2006) *Addiction Counselling*. Melbourne: IP Communications.

McGill, T. (2006) *Dealing with Drugs*. Elstrenwick: Insight Publications.

McKenna, C. (2002) "Ecstasy is low in league table of major causes of deaths." *British Medical Journal 325*, 296.

McNeel, J.R. (1980) "The parent interview." *Transactional Analysis Journal 6*, 1, 61–68.

Medical Dictionary (2011) "Locus of control." Available at http://medical-dictionary.thefreedictionary.com/locus+of+control, accessed May 2, 2012.

Midgley, D. (1993) "Character disorder—A transactional analysis perspective." *ITA News 36*, 4–6.

Miller, W. (1983) "Motivational interviewing with problem drinkers." *Behavioural Psychotherapy 11*, 147–172.

Moss, J. (1982) "Relationships: The dependency trap." *New Parent 4*, 4–7.

Nutt, D., King, L.A., Saulsbury, W., and Blakemore, C. (2007) "Development of a rational scale to assess the harm of drugs of potential misuse." *Lancet 369*, 24, 1047–1053.

O'Callaghan, F., Sonderegger, N., and Klag, S. (2004) "Drug and crime cycle: Evaluating traditional methods versus diversion strategies for drug-related offences." *Australian Psychologist 39*, 188–200.

O'Connor, J. (1996) "Addiction as a psychological process." In C. Wilkinson and B. Saunders (eds) *Perspectives on Addiction*. Perth: William Montgomery.

Piaget, J. and Inhelder, B (1969) *The Psychology of the Child*. New York: Basic Books.

Pickering, M. (1972) "Memoirs of a kif smoker." In G. Andrews and S. Vinkenoog (eds) *The Book of Grass: An Anthology of Indian Hemp*. Ringwood: Penguin Books.

Polster, E. and Polster, M. (1973) *Gestalt Therapy Integrated*. New York: Vintage Books.

Prochaska, J.O. and DiClemente, C.C. (1982) "Transtheoretical therapy: Toward a more integrative model of change." *Psychotherapy: Theory, Research and Practice 19*, 276–288.

Reich, W. (1972) *Character Analysis*. New York: Farrar, Straus and Giroux.

Reinhart, D.F. and Edwards, C.E. (2009) "Childhood physical and verbal mistreatment, psychological symptoms, and substance use: Sex differences and the moderating role of attachment." *Journal of Family Violence 24*, 589–596.

Rotter, J.B. (1966) "Generalized expectancies for internal versus external control of reinforcement." *Psychological Monographs 80*, 1–28.

Rutter, M., Kreppner, J., and Sonuga-Barke, E. (2009) "Emanuel Miller lecture: Attachment insecurity, disinhibited attachment, and attachment disorders: where do research findings leave the concepts?" *Journal of Child Psychology and Psychiatry 50*, 529–543.

Saunders, W. and Wilkinson, C. (1990) "Motivation and addiction behavior: A psychological perspective." *Drug and Alcohol Review 9*, 133–142.

Sherwan, D. and Dalgarno, P. (2005) "Evidence for controlled heroin use? Low levels of negative health and social outcomes among non-treatment heroin users in Glasgow (Scotland)." *British Journal of Health Psychology 10*, 33–48.

Simkin, J.S. (1974) *Mini-Lectures in Gestalt Therapy*. Albany, California: Wordpress.

Steinberg, L. (2011) *You and Your Adolescent*. New York: Simon and Schuster.

Steiner, C. (1971) *Games Alcoholics Play*. New York: Grove Press.

Stewart, I. and Joines, V. (1987) *TA Today*. Nottingham: Lifespace Publishing.

The Australian. (1997) Heroin. Page 11. News Corporation.

Treatment Protocol Project (2004) *Management of Mental Disorders*, 4th edn. Sydney: World Health Organization Collaborating Centre for Evidence in Mental Health Policy.

Tucker, P. (2009) "Substance misuse and early psychosis." *Australasian Psychiatry* *17*, 4, 291–294.

Vaillant, G. and Milofsky, E. (1982) "Natural history of male alcoholism IV: Paths to recovery." *Archives of General Psychiatry 39*, 127–133.

Walker, T. (2012) "The new ages of man." Available at www.independent.co.uk/life-style/health-and-families/features/the-new-ages-of-man-7537626.html, accessed on May 11, 2012.

Western Australian Police Service (1996) *Drug Information Booklet.* Perth: Health Department of Western Australia.

White, T. (1990a) "The infant ballet." *Mind: The Magazine of Human Behaviour 7*, 4.

White, T. (1990b) *Adolescence, Anger and What to Do: A Happy Teenager is Not a Healthy Teenager.* Perth: T.A. Books.

White, T. (1997a) "Symbiosis and attachment hunger." *Transactional Analysis Journal 27*, 300–304.

White, T. (1997b) "Is a happy teenager a healthy teenager: Four levels of adolescent anger." *Transactional Analysis Journal 27*, 192–196.

White, T. (1997c) "Heroin use as a passive behaviour." *Drugwise: Official Publication for the Palmerston Association* (Autumn), 25.

White, T. (1998) "Transference, attachment and the transactional symbiosis." *Transactional Analysis Journal 28*, 121–126.

White, T. (1999) "Heroin use as a passive behaviour." *Transactional Analysis Journal 29*, 273–277.

White, T. (2010) "Cannabis and self medication." Available at http://graffiti99.blogspot.com/2010/07/cannabis-and-self-medication.html, accessed May 2, 2012.

White, T. (2011) *Working with Suicidal Individuals: A Guide to Providing Understanding, Assessment and Support.* London: Jessica Kingsley Publishers.

Wilkinson, C. and Saunders, B. (1996) (eds.) *Perspectives On Addiction.* Perth: William Montgomery.

Winick, C. (1962) "Maturing out of narcotic addiction." *UN Bulletin of Narcotics 16*, 107–121.

Woollams, S. and Brown, M. (1978) *Transactional Analysis.* Michigan: Huron Valley Institute Press.

Further Reading

More on transactional analysis can be found in *TA Today* by I. Stewart and V. Joines, published by Lifespace Publishing (Nottingham) in 1987, and *Talking TA* by L. Cameron, published by WPATA Publications (Perth, Australia) in 1988.

Further reading on drug and alcohol use and abuse and transactional analysis can also be found on Tony White's website: www.ynot1.com.au, and weblog: http://graffiti99.blogspot.com. These sites include regularly updated lists of articles and comments, as well as some cutting-edge thinking on these three areas.

Any comments or questions on drug and alcohol use and abuse and transactional analysis can be directed to the author, Tony White, at: Western Institute, 136 Loftus Street, North Perth, 6006, Western Australia, Australia; email: agbw@bigpond.com.

Index

urine testing 34–6, 208–9

Vaillant, G. 91
valium
 clearance time from urine 35
Vanhaeghe, P. 63
Vanheule, S. 63
Vink, J.M. 29

Walker, T. 186
Western Australian Drug Users and
 AIDS Association 35
Western Australian Police Service 205
White, T. 32, 33, 55, 57, 61, 82, 104, 111,
 113, 114, 133, 186, 203
Wilkinson, C. 57, 171
Winick, C. 87
Woollams, S. 48

young people
 and harm minimization 117–19 *see also*
 teenagers